D1153114

This book is to
the la.. d.

BOOKS OVERDUE

A

Women in Uniform
through the centuries

Frontispiece   Queen Victoria, *c.* 1840. An artist's design for a uniform

Women
in Uniform

through the centuries

Elizabeth Ewing

B. T. Batsford Ltd

London & Sydney

To Nicola Milligan SRN, SCM, HV
who has worn nine uniforms

First published 1975
© Elizabeth Ewing 1975
ISBN 0 7134 2996 8

Filmset by Keyspools Ltd, Golborne, Lancashire
Printed and bound in Great Britain by
The Pitman Press, Bath
for the publishers B. T. Batsford Ltd,
4 Fitzhardinge Street, London WIH OAH
& 23 Cross Street, Brookvale, NSW 2100
Australia

Contents

List of Illustrations

Acknowledgments

Special thanks must be accorded to the staffs of the Royal Library, Windsor; the British Library; the London Library and the libraries of the Fawcett Society; the Imperial War Museum; the London College of Fashion; the National Army Museum; the National Maritime Museum; the Old War Office; the Royal College of Nursing and the Victoria and Albert Museum.

Valuable help has been given to me by Mrs Barbara Acton, of the Costume Society of Scotland; Mr William G. T. Boag, Assistant Keeper of the Scottish United Services Museum; Miss Edith Cross, Archivist of the North London Collegiate School, and Miss Miriam Shillito, Assistant Archivist; Lady (Betty) Cuthbert, formerly Chief Woman Officer of the NFS; Miss Daphne Edmonds, Keeper of the Department of Uniforms, National Army Museum; Miss Catharine and Miss Isabel Ewing; Miss V. M. Garner, MBE, Assistant Inspector of Fire Services; Mr Charles H. Gibbs-Smith; Miss Hazel Goddard, of the British Women Pilots' Association; Head Deaconess Ann Gurney; Miss N. S. Hancock of the Princess Christian College; Mrs J. E. Kelley, Assistant Director in Charge of Women's Prison Service; Miss Jean S. Law, OBE, Assistant Inspector of Constabulary, Home Office; Mr Dan Ivall, OBE, formerly Assistant Inspector of Fire Services; Miss Veronica Humphrey, Wardrobe Mistress, Christ's Hospital, Hertford; Miss W. L. Huntly, Archivist of the London Hospital; Mrs Laura C. Le Maitre, of St Leonards School; First Officer Jill McDougall, of the WRNS; Miss Gillian Mackay, Chairman of the British Women Pilots' Association; Mr R. W. Sharpington, of St Thomas's Hospital; Miss Prunella Stack, of the Women's League of Health and Beauty; Miss M. I. Taylor, of the Girls' Brigade; Squadron Leader Valerie Webster, of the WRAF; Lieut.-Col. D. C. Weeks, RAMC, of the Royal Army Medical College; Mrs Mavis Wilson and Mr Terence Wise.

Finally, grateful thanks are due to Miriam Wessel, Douglas Sellick and Michael Stephenson, of B. T. Batsford, who have helped immeasurably in the planning and execution of this book, and to Kathleen Bawden, who brought unstinted care and patience to typing it.

1 | Beginnings

Uniformity is not natural to humankind, but everywhere people are in uniform. Few of those living in the western world today have not worn it at some time, yet to many it seems an aberration from that uniqueness of the individual which is his highest quality. 'The worst feature of a life of routine is, of course, that it smears us into uniformity,' said Sir Mortimer Wheeler in a different context than that of clothes but with equal relevance. In Utopia there would be no uniforms – but equally there would be none in a completely chaotic society. Between these hypothetical states the community exerts its influence on all its members. Interdependence is a law of life and costume throughout its history has been an expression of the shared needs, tastes and attitudes, conscious or unrealised, of people in a community. They dress in certain ways at any given time and change at varying speeds, a process which goes by the name of fashion.

Fashion is usually established by the dominant group in the community and is then taken up by whatever other sections of the populace have the freedom and the will to do so – and keeping up with the Joneses is a strong social urge. There is therefore in all fashion a slant towards uniformity as part of the life of any community with a claim to being orderly. Costume moves out of this, its ordinary and natural context, and into uniforms when a section of the community stands apart, voluntarily or by compulsion, for some specific purpose and identifies this by adopting a distinctive mode of dress. It follows from this that the history of women in uniform is closely bound up with their position in the community. 'Women don't live in a vacuum; they live in society,' said Jennie Lee in 1941. It was true then and it is true now, but for centuries women did live in a vacuum so far as large areas of personal and communal activity were concerned. Their wearing of uniform is closely connected with their movement into the community. It is in some ways a pictorial story of their progress.

Whatever they are and whatever course they follow, uniforms, both men's and women's, are a special part of social history, as well as part of costume history. They are normally based on or derived from a contemporary fashion, but they become frozen in their particular mode, adopted to indicate their particular function but continuing long after the fashion itself has changed.

As uniforms denote a distinction and a function to be performed, their origins must lie where this was first expressed. One area was the very basic one of the division between master and servant. Power, wealth and authority were shown by grand dressing, the outward and visible signs of the assertion of the individual. Kings and queens wore crowns and special robes, noblemen developed their own insignia, military leaders went into spectacular uniforms. Conversely, the lower orders lacked all these things. Restrictions and rules about their clothing were one form of the denial of individual rights which is slavery or servitude – and this led to another interpretation of uniforms.

In ancient Egypt the slave or servant was designated by a lack of clothing rather than by any distinguishing livery. 'The wearing of clothes,' says James Laver of this stage of society, 'was a kind of class distinction.' In Greece and Rome things were less drastic, but the principle was the same: the lower the status the fewer and rougher were the clothes. Servants and slaves in Greece were forbidden to wear coloured clothes. A kind of neutral reddish brown was the main attire of the poor and it is paralleled by the women's 'russet' gowns frequently referred to in the middle ages and later in the context of servants' clothing – an approach towards uniform. Similar to this was the 'hodden grey' of an early tradition which extends almost to our own day, mainly in connection with working gear. Herodotus refers to an Athenian edict forbidding the poor to appear in dyed clothes at the theatre or other public places. The Roman toga was denied to respectable women and to slaves but, oddly, was the badge of the prostitute.

Since fashion, as we understand it, did not exist in those days, when draped robes were worn by all, with little change for centuries, uniform at this stage could not be very sharply distinguished in any social or other groups. But a few small, intriguing items come up to its definition by the Concise Oxford Dictionary as 'dress worn by members of same body', among them the elaborate sandals displayed by the top ladies among the Greek *hetairai*, or call girls. Later fashion produced similar distinctions. The Venetian *Cortigiane* wore a special costume by regulation and in Cosimo's Florence a yellow veil was prescribed for light ladies. Masks were originally introduced by Venetian courtesans, red shoes had a like significance at one time in Italy and high-laced, tightly fitting boots were a hallmark of the street-walker up to Victorian days.

It was, however, for a high and serious purpose that the first and longest-lasting of all women's uniforms in the Oxford Dictionary's sense came into being. Although the course of men's and women's uniforms was subsequently to follow some very different lines, with those of men taking an irrecoverable, spectacular and unchallenged lead, both in number and variety, the two were at an early stage closely linked in religious communities. The plain, severe habits enjoined for wear by monks and nuns

1   Plain severe habits were the uniforms of early nuns

dedicated to a life of prayer, charitable works and renunciation of the world are the first established uniforms of our epoch, dating from the early centuries of the Christian era. The earliest religious women were called deaconesses and one of them is mentioned by St Paul in his Epistle to the Romans as 'a servant of the church'. The early deaconesses ranked with the clergy, and were also the first parish workers and district nurses, mainly in the East. They were not organised into communities, and prob ably did not wear uniform, but they were the predecessors of the later communities of nuns who wore distinctive dress and who were well established by the sixth century. The order of deaconesses was revived in the nineteenth century with uniforms.

The existence of communities of nuns is recorded by St Jerome in the fourth century and in the fifth by St Augustine, who was welcomed at Thanet by King Ethelbert of Kent and his wife Bertha, a Christian who directed such a community. Monks and nuns lived under closely similar conditions from this time and the robes they wore were based on the contemporary Anglo-Saxon dress of the early centuries, when traditional long, loose robes were generally worn. The habit of the nun, as of the monk, was part of their Rule, 'so there is reluctance to change or modify it', says Suzanne Cito-Malard in *Religious Orders of Women*. 'Those designed precisely as religious garb (and not, for instance, in imitation of an Italian widow's mourning dress or a French chatelaine's working costume),' she continues, 'have endured longest in their original design.' Of religious habits, she explains, those of Benedictines, Dominicans, Poor Clares and Carmelites were monastic in origin, meant as the 'uniform' of women consecrated to God. Others with sweeping trains, complicated headdresses or intricately-pleated skirts, had links with secular fashion. They were therefore more subject to modification.

The elaborate headdresses of nuns also began as part of the dress of the time, many of the shapes being a perpetuation of medieval fashion. The ceremonies of consecration and of the veil were established at an early date. The great vogue of the veil, both among religious women and in the world outside, has also been linked with the Crusades, being seen as an adaptation by western women of an Eastern custom which went back to Assyria about 1200 BC. The choice of black, or dark, muted colours for the robes of the religious orders was a symbol of their renunciation of the sensual world.

The nun's wimple, a neck-covering which was draped over the bosom, round the neck and then drawn up to frame the face, and pinned on the top of the head under the veil, was a generally worn fashion from the middle of the twelfth century and lasted for about two centuries. After that it was confined to widows, for a time, and to women of the religious orders, some of whom wear it to this day. The barbette, a band worn round or over the temples, dates from about the same time, and it too was a secular fashion perpetuated by the religious orders.

Double monasteries and nunneries, often both under the supreme rule

2 The habit of women members of the early Order of St John

3 Almost identical was the timeless dress of the Benedictine nun

4 Uniformity among nuns of La Sainte Abbaye, *c*. 1300

of an abbess, were frequent in Britain in Anglo-Saxon times, being introduced about the fourth century from Gaul and Ireland. The abbesses, the first women to achieve equal status with men, were of royal or noble birth, prominent among them being St Etheldreda of Ely, St Mildred of Thanet and St Hilda of Whitby. These, and many others comparable to them, exercised a profound influence; Anglo-Saxon women enjoyed an authority which had no parallel until recent days. The peak of this female learning and power in the nunnery was reached in the sixth and seventh centuries, and the most notable of all the learned ladies in uniform was St Hilda. Born in 614, she was the daughter of King Edwin of Northumbria and her responsibilities extended beyond her 'black-robed monks and nuns' to include a considerable population living on the Abbey lands.

Some of the outstanding religious women of these centuries 'had rank and ecclesiastical as barons and peers'. A few of them attended the Saxon parliament, the Witenagamot, thus providing a nice precedent for the 1918 Act empowering women to sit in the House of Commons – as was pointed out at that time to answer protests against women securing the vote and the right to become MP's.

In addition to their erudition and sanctity, the early religious women were also the first teachers of girls, whose education was entirely in their hands for centuries and remained so to a considerable degree until the Reformation. St Hilda has been described as the first great English woman teacher and 1200 years later she was the ideal revered by Dorothea Beale, probably the greatest single force in the development of modern education for girls. Education in early times was, however, limited to girls of high rank.

The nunnery as the centre of education declined in the centuries immediately before the Reformation. This was partly because the foundation of the universities and grammar schools for boys was channelling off learning from the church. But, in addition, with the growing

5 English Abbess of later 13th–early 14th century

sophistication of high life and the cult of romantic love, girls were being educated in 'accomplishments' rather than in the straight and narrow path of convent learning. Chaucer in his *Physician's Tale* advises girls' teachers to teach 'vertu', and romantic tales like *Troilus and Cressida* and *Lancelot and Guinevere* were spreading sentimental ideals. Education from about the ninth century passed increasingly into the Palace schools. Charlemagne pioneered this trend in the eighth century, and his daughters were brought up with their brothers at court, by men and women teachers.

As the elegancies of life became more important for girls, needlework and art were increasingly taught, both in nunneries and at court. This had an effect on the character of the nuns – and on their break from strict rules of dress. Chaucer's Prioress is one classic example of how far religious women had moved from the old austere Saxon tradition. With her airs and graces, her elaborate table manners, Madame Eglentyne is treated with gentle irony. Her tears are for the 'mous caught in a trappe', not for the great sufferings of humanity, and her devotion goes to her 'smale houndes . . . that she fedde with roasted flesh or milk and wastelbreed'. She is elegantly dressed too:

> *Ful fetis was her cloke, as I was war.*
> *Of smal coral about hir arm she bar*
> *A peire of bedes gauded all with grene;*
> *And ther-on heng a broche of gold full shene,*
> *On which there was first write a crowned A,*
> *And after, Amor vincit omnia.*

It is a far step from the religious 'uniform'. Strictly speaking, she should not have been allowed to desert the cloister at all to go on the pilgrimage, but this had become common.

The records of the later middle ages abound in evidence of the three centuries' long battle waged by the ruling ecclesiastics, men by now, to control the worldly excesses of the nuns, who were in revolt against their prescribed uniform and, indeed, against most of the tenets of the religious life. Such a life had ceased to have either significance or purpose; so had its uniform.

In 1200 the Council of London had sought to restrain the black nuns from wearing coloured headdress. The standard decree on the subject was issued at Oxford in 1222 by the Council, which had laid down that 'Since it is necessary that the female sex, so weak against the wiles of the ancient enemy, should be fortified by many reminders, we decree that nuns and other women dedicated to divine worship shall not wear a silken wimple, nor dare to carry silver or golden tiring pins in their veil. Neither shall they . . . wear belts of silk, or adorned with gold or silver, nor henceforth use burnet or any other unlawful cloth. . . . Also let them measure their gown according to the dimensions of their body, so that it does not exceed the length of the body.' A 1237 synod said: 'We forbid to . . . nuns coloured garments or bedclothes, save those dyed black. . . . And nuns are not to use trained or pleated dresses, or any exceeding the length of the body, nor delicate or coloured furs.' This was repeated almost word for word by William of Wykham in injunctions issued to Romsey and Wherwell in 1387, and other similar orders abound, including one that the veil was not to be used 'to adorn their countenances by spreading it in a becoming fashion'. Large collars, laced shoes and elaborate girdles were forbidden and nuns at Witherfoss in 1318 were ordered not to wear red dresses and long supertunics 'like secular women'. Silk clothes and veils, rich furs, rings, brooches and silver and gilt pins all came in for condemnation. In 1249 at a French nunnery at Rouen it is said that 'they all wear their hair long to their chins', and at another 'nuns wore ringlets'. At Romsey in 1502 the commissionary of the Prior of Canterbury found that two nuns 'wore their hair long'.

This movement out of uniform is detailed by Eileen Power in *Medieval English Nunneries*. She tells of accusations of wearing rich clothing brought against Clemence Medforde, Prioress of Ankerwyke, in 1442, when 'The Prioresse wears golden rings exceedingly costly with divers precious stones, and also girdles silvered and gilded over and silken veils. . . . Also she wears kirtles faced with silk and tiring pins of silver and silver gilt and has made all the nuns wear the like.' There were even complaints made about nuns that their 'nails, like those of a falcon or sparrow hawk, are pared to resemble talons'. For centuries, Miss Powell concludes, 'synods sat solemnly over silken veils and pleated robes with long trains. . . . For three weary centuries bishops waged a holy war against fashion in the cloister and waged it in vain.'

How convent education and those who provided and received it had declined is illustrated by Chaucer's *Reve's Tale*, in which the wife of Simkin the miller, who is 'pert as is a pye', (repellant) 'smoterliche' (of dubious reputation) and 'digne as water in a ditch', is ironically described as of noble birth because 'the person of the town hir fader was', and because she was 'yfostered in a nonnerie'. Uniforms persisted, however, in the poor nunneries – and there were many of them, proceeding towards new developments. In 1390 a citizen of York, Roger de Noreton, said in his will: 'I bequeath to my daughter a nun of St Clement's, York, to buy her blak flannels . . . according to her needs, four marks of silver.' Sir Thomas Cumberworth, who died in 1451, directed that 've blak Curteynes of lawne be cut in vailes and gyfyn to poore nones'.

While nunneries declined as a main stronghold of religion and of female learning and education, they continued to be an important source of the first and greatest of women's vocations and one associated with the wearing of distinguishing uniforms right up to our own day – that of nursing. The bearing and rearing of children links women inalienably with the preservation of life and therefore with the care of the sick and the frail. There have been women nurses since the earliest recorded history. The first to have left her name and fame in history-cum-legend is Hygieia, one of the daughters of Aesclepius, first of the great Greek healers, whom she helped in the rites of his temple, as did her sisters, Iaso, Panacea and Ayle. Women are recorded in the *Odyssey* and the *Iliad* as giving medical aid, chief of them being the *Iliad*'s 'yellow-haired Agamede, who knew as many drugs as the wide earth nourishes' – though perhaps she should be ranked as the first woman doctor.

After the fall of the Greek civilisation, the caliphs in the Mohammedan world revived medicine and founded hospitals as well as the libraries for which they are more famous. All their great towns had infirmaries and dispensaries, where knowledge and skill were of a high standard. With the growth of the Christian faith in the western world and of the compassion for the afflicted which was a profound part of it, the care of the sick came under the chief upholders of religion, the monks and nuns. Monasteries and nunneries had their own hospitals, primarily for the care of their own members but, as religious houses were the first hotels and lodging houses for travellers, their scope was extended to such arrivals. The charitable work of the religious orders among the community also brought the poor under their care.

The important part played by women in religious life meant that they were closely involved in tending the sick and in the development of hospitals. The oldest purely nursing order in existence is that of the Hôtel-Dieu of Paris, founded in AD 650 and consisting of nuns belonging to the Augustinian sisterhood. At times nuns from the Hôtel-Dieu nursed at Barts and St Thomas's Hospitals in London. The first English hospitals, as distinct from the infirmaries of convents or monasteries, came into existence in the twelfth century. St Bartholomews, or Barts, was founded in 1123, St Mary's in 1197 and St Thomas's in 1215. Like the hospitals of religious houses, they were in early days under the care of monks and nuns and for about 1,000 years, from the fifth century AD, men and women of the religious orders ranked as equals in importance in maintaining what we would today call hospital services. In the twelfth century Queen Matilda set up the hospital of St Giles in the East, where she herself nursed, and where she also set up the order of Poor Clares, to serve in the wards. It still exists and wears a uniform of medieval austerity.

With the Reformation and the dissolution of the monasteries the nurses continued to be called Sisters, in the old religious tradition, and the religious precedent of a woman being in all-over charge, which stemmed from the double monasteries under the supreme rule of an abbess, was also maintained by the installation of a matron in charge – another tradition which has remained unbroken.

Matron and Sisters were from this time paid board wages and also an allowance for their 'liverie'. This is on record as consisting of 'a kertyll and a petycote and a kertyll and a wastcote', which were made for the staff of Barts at a charge of 20 pence in 1544. The first matron, Rose Fyssher, who is mentioned in 1551, wore workaday russet frieze to start with, but changed to watchet or light blue, the colour also adopted in a different tone by the Sisters. Such a blue has to this day remained the dominant choice for all kinds of nurses' uniforms, including those at Barts. There is a further sixteenth-century record of a yearly allocation of six yards of russet frieze, later also changed to watchet, for nurses' uniforms at Barts. Headdresses followed the fashion of the day, which was for the head to be covered indoors by a cap. In 1686 the governors of Barts presented 'night rales' (cloaks) and hoods of white linen to their nurses.

A 'livery' was always regarded as necessary, and failure to wear it meant dismissal. Cloth continued to be supplied by Barts, as by other hospitals, and the 'night rales' remained in existence till 1843, when the Sisters were still in blue, but assistant nurses in brown. The cloak, still widely worn by nurses today, is thus the longest-lasting as well as a very distinctive item of nurses' uniform, worn in short, long and shoulder-length versions, with little change through the centuries that have seen the uniform dress go through a hundred variations.

The importance of these post-reformation hospitals is that they marked the beginning of lay nursing and civilian control of hospitals but at the same time, by virtue of religious associations and traditions, carried within them the sense of dedication, the over-ruling spirit of service which was to be deeply imbued in the nursing profession in its future progress. The wearing of uniform has always been, to the wearers and to the world for which they work, a symbol of this spirit – a spirit felt by other, later uniformed groups of women but supremely potent here.

Meantime, however, nursing was to go through its 'dark ages' of more than two centuries, when, in the stress of warfare, civil strife and social upheaval, the status of the nurse fell to a level that had not been experienced for centuries. Traditions and training lapsed, most hospitals reached depths of squalor and the idea of the sick poor being the responsibility of the community was lost. Uniforms went into abeyance. Until well into the nineteenth century the image of the nurse perpetuated by Dickens

"Copyright" by permission of Messrs. Chapman & Hall London.

7   Sarah Gamp. Uniforms have disappeared. From *Martin Chuzzlewit*

in Sarah Gamp and Betsy Trott in *Martin Chuzzlewit* and *David Copper-field* was only too real. The gin-sodden reprobate was typical of the only type of woman who could be found to undertake nursing. It fell below the lowest grade of domestic service, so appalling were the conditions of most hospitals. A very few Anglican sisterhoods and still fewer surviving Roman Catholic ones remained and it was these which kept alive a faint spark to be re-lit by Florence Nightingale, and a tradition of uniformed nursing devotion to be revived as part of her vast achievement.

2 | Service and servitude

8 Working dress, but not
uniform, for the woman servant,
as seen by Chardin (1699–1779)

Women in domestic service might well seem likely to be early starters and
leaders in the story of uniforms, but that is not so. The strictness of their
dress is almost wholly Victorian in origin and until then it showed great
variety. Almost the only item to be generally worn was the apron, and it
was not exclusive to them. It is on record in pictures from the thirteenth
century onwards, being also called 'aperne' and 'napron'. It was first
worn by men, among them artisans, builders, general workers and cooks,
but women also appear in it from the early fourteenth century. In most
cases they are countrywomen or servants and the typical apron was large,
bibless, tied round the waist and often trimmed with a band of embroidery
below the waist. It was usually made of coarse linen, for protection. When,
in 1825, Samuel and Sarah Adams wrote *The Complete Servant*, the first
detailed book on the relations between masters and servants, they dealt
with men servants' uniforms in some detail, but to the woman servant
their only advice was that she should be neat and clean and proceed in-
dustriously from one job to another 'having washed her hands and put on a
clean apron' with some frequency. Hannah Woolley, who wrote on
servant problems at the end of the seventeenth century, limited her advice
to the woman servant on dress to seeing that she was attired 'neatly, titely
and cleanly' after doing the rough work.

Women servants usually wore a rougher version of current fashion, the
materials being those of the rest of the lower orders, including homespun,
frieze, kersey, kendal, russet, fustian and even sackcloth for outer garments and coarse linen for underwear. The universal ground-length

skirts were worn even by labouring women, but were sometimes turned up into a waist-belt, leaving the petticoat to bear the brunt of dirt and damp. This became a feature of women household servants' attire. The 'dark stuff gown' often mentioned in records as typical servants' wear was probably the precursor of the universal black of the Victorian servants' formal uniform and, like it, thought suitable for the subdued lower orders.

Several factors conspired against the woman domestic servant being given a specific uniform. Firstly, the main purpose of servants' uniforms was to demonstrate the wealth and importance of their masters and among the well-heeled the servants who appeared in public were almost all men until well into the eighteenth century and in many cases much later. They were therefore put into liveries which were a matter of great concern and of which many details survive. Women servants worked mainly behind the scenes in subordinate positions, so that they were not dressed for show. The cap usually worn was not distinctive, as head coverings were worn indoors by both men and women for centuries and women continued to be thus covered until the late nineteenth century. By the 1890s only elderly women and domestic servants wore caps, but many a dignified dowager had a confection of lace and ribbons atop her head in the early years of this century, rivalled only by her smart parlour-maid. Uniform was, as often, perpetuating fashion.

Another reason for the lack of uniforms among women servants was that until the invention of the sewing machine in the mid-nineteenth century the making of clothes was a laborious matter and the mistress normally handed on her clothes to her servants. Dorothy Margaret Stuart, tracing the history of the woman domestic servant in *The English Abigail*, unearthed many old wills showing that from the thirteenth century women servants were frequently bequeathed clothes by their employers. Sarah, Duchess of Marlborough, said in her will that her wardrobe was to be divided between her lady's maid and two other maid servants. Richardson's heroine, Pamela, was presented with many rich items of wear which had belonged to her dead employer, a usual procedure.

A further factor was that women servants if not too humble were too exalted to wear uniform. At one extreme an early thirteenth century writer, describes the servant woman who is 'put in office and werke of traveylle, toylynge and slubberynge', fed on 'grosse mete and symple' and 'kept lowe under the yolke of thraldom and of servage'. At the other extreme there are maids in Elizabethan and Jacobean plays who are the confidantes of their mistresses, like the 'maid to Isabella' in the *Spanish Tragedy* or Carola in *The Duchess of Malfi*, who shares the secret of her mistress's marriage to the faithful steward. Maria in *Twelfth Night* marries Sir Toby Belch and this is not regarded as an unusual match for Viola's pert maid.

Though women servants were slow to go into uniform, they were frequently recruited from one of the earliest and youngest groups of their

9   The Lady's maid, 1841, too grand to wear uniform

10   Statue of seventeenth century Bluecoat girl at Christ's Hospital

sex to do so. Women servants were often charity or workhouse girls who were 'apprenticed' in this way. Defoe's Moll Flanders, for instance, was a poor-law child who, after being threatened with domestic service at the age of eight, became companion-attendant to the daughter of a lady at the age of 14.

The social problem presented by orphaned or deserted children was an acute one and the first stirrings of compassion led to the setting up of 'hospitals' for their relief and of endowments made for this purpose from the sixteenth century. Distinctive uniforms were usually worn by these children. The first such hospital, Christ's Hospital, was the result of a sermon preached in 1552 by Nicholas Ridley, Bishop of London, which moved the boy king Edward VI to support a scheme for setting up an institution for 'poor fatherless children'. At the opening of the school in 1553 at Greyfriars Monastery, the girls wore a uniform of 'russet cotton with kerchiefs on their heads', but by Easter day they had assumed the uniform which, basically unchanged, continued to be worn until 1875. This consisted of a blue dress, a white, green or blue apron, white coif and peak (hat) and usually yellow stockings. They were known as Bluecoat girls and the boys as Bluecoat boys.

The two schools, for boys and girls, still exist under their original names. The girls' one, at Hertford, is the oldest boarding school for girls, with a continuous history moving upward educationally until today it holds a high place in the educational world. The uniform is now smart and up-to-date, but it can claim to be derived from the first of all school uniforms. Two coloured statues of Bluecoat girls in their seventeenth-century uniform were set up in two niches in the outside walls of the eighteenth-century girls' schoolroom at Hertford, to which it had moved, and they are still there, bright and shining in new paint. Replicas of the original dress are treasured in the school wardrobe department and are worn for commemorative occasions. The school museum has miniatures of dresses of various periods and dolls wearing the original dress, as well as a set of sketches showing the dress in detail – the oldest non-religious women's uniform on record.

John Evelyn described the school in March 1657: 'There were near 800 boys and girls so decently clad, cleanly lodg'd, so wholesomely fed, so admirably taught . . . that I was delighted to see the progress. . . . The girls were instructed in all such work as becomes their sex, and may fit them for good wives, mistresses and to be a blessing to their generation.' Pepys, who was a Governor of the Hospital, has a charming story, told in a letter to Mrs Steward, dated 20 September 1695, of two wealthy citizens leaving their estates, one to a Blue Coat boy, and the other to a Blue Coat girl, in Christ's Hospital. This extraordinary circumstance led the magistrates to arrange a match 'which is ended in a public wedding, he in his habit of blue satin, led by two of the girls, and she in blue, with an apron green and petticoat yellow, all of sarsnet, led by two of the boys of the House through Cheapside to Guildhall Chapel, where they were married by the Dean of

St Paul's, she given by my Lord Mayor'. Unfortunately no entry to this effect can be traced in Guildhall Chapel or in the children's register, but it must have been the first wedding in which both bride and groom wore uniform – and it would be centuries before it was repeated, probably by the Salvation Army and then by servicewomen of World War One.

It was part of the policy of those responsible for the charity schools that the boys and girls, wearing their distinctive uniforms, should take part in ceremonials and public events in the City of London. The diarist Henry Manchyn describes the four hundred 'men and women chyldren, all in blue cotes, and menssys (wenches) in blue frokes, and with skaychons inbrodered on their slevys with the armes of London and red capes' at a public ceremony at the beginning of the seventeenth century. It is also recorded that in 1604 James I and his Queen, Anne of Denmark, 'were saluted with song by three hundred children of Christ's Hospital ranged on a platform in Barking Churchyard'. The girls also performed a masque before Anne of Denmark on 4 May 1617.

Alderman John Whitson of Bristol established an early charity school in that city, where 40 daughters of freemen were to be educated and maintained. Due to a stipulation in his will in 1627 that they were to be 'apparelled in red cloth', they became known as the Red Maids. The eighteenth century was, however, the great era of expansion of the charity school movement, with its compulsory uniforms. The industrial revolution had produced appalling conditions for poor children and the betterment of their condition was one main activity of the Society for the Propagation of Christian Knowledge, founded in 1698, with a similar society established in Scotland in 1700.

Bishop Butler referred in St Paul's to 'the various coloured coats and kirtles of the "Clothed children", garments which by making the wearers public objects of charity did nothing to encourage vanity and reminded them continually of their servile rank'. The effigy of a charity child, usually a girl, in uniform was sometimes set up at the door of a church or school with a poor box beside it inviting contributions. The subordination of charity children was felt to be commendable and their uniform was part of it. Isaac Watts in *An Essay towards the Encouragement of Charity Schools* said in 1728: 'Their clothes are of the coarsest kind, and of the plainest form, thus they are sufficiently distinguished from the children of the better rank, and they ought to be distinguished. . . . There is no ground for charity children to grow vain and proud of their rayment when it is but a sort of livery.'

The do-gooders drew great satisfaction from the sight of charity children on official occasions. Thus in March 1703 the committee of the SPCK mooted the idea 'that the Poor Children in all the Charity Schools might walk in Procession once a year to some Church and there heare a Sermon'. The first of these took place in Whitsun week, 1704, in St Andrew's Church, Holborn. As the number of charity children grew, a special charity sermon was preached annually at St Paul's by a leading

11 Charity children going to church at Kirkby, Notts. in 1786

divine. Scholars also paraded on many great occasions, 'new cloath'd and singing lustily', according to one record. On a day of thanksgiving for peace with France a huge scaffolding 600 feet long was set up in the Strand to accommodate 4,000 charity children, boys and girls, in full view of the procession. Joseph Addison in 1715 was greatly affected by the 'innocent multitude' which formed 'a spectacle pleasing both to God and Man' on another occasion, and he found charity schools 'the glory of the Age we live in'. Blake, in his *Songs of Innocence*, has an enchanting picture of these uniformed children in 1789:

> '*Twas on a Holy Thursday, their innocent faces clean,*
> *The children walking two and two, in red and blue and green,*
> *Grey-headed beadles walk'd before, with wands as white as snow*
> *Till into the high dome of Paul's, they like Thames' waters flow,*
> *O what a multitude they seem'd, these flowers of London town,*
> *Seated in companies they sit with radiance all their own,*
> *The hum of multitudes was there, but multitudes of lambs,*
> *Thousands of little boys and girls, raising their innocent hands.*

Other references record with pride the sight of the charity children: 'There is a natural Beauty in Uniformity which most People delight in,' says De Mandeville. 'It is diverting to the Eye to see Children well match'd, either Boys or Girls, march two and two in good Order; and to have there all whole and light in the same Cloaths and Trimmings must add to the Comeliness of the Sight.'

Charity schools proliferated in the eighteenth century, among the most famous being Capt Coram's Bloomsbury Foundling Hospital, founded in 1739, and the Greycoat School, founded in York in the early eighteenth century, both of them with distinctive uniforms. Girls at such schools were trained mainly for domestic service, until enlightened women raised protests against the neglect of their general education. But even the humane Mrs Trimmer in her *Oeconomy of Charity* approved of carding, spinning, sewing and knitting for five-year-olds and a 1723 attack on charity schools provoked a storm of protests to the effect that 'any wise Person' would prefer a servant from a charity school than from a poor home, the difference being as much 'as is a tamed from a wild beast'. Poor little *madchen* in uniform.

With the eighteenth century's commercial and industrial expansion servants became very numerous, especially among the rising middle classes. Parson Woodforde on £300 a year had five, three men and two women. Horace Walpole's friend Mary Berry estimated in 1796 that to live comfortably in London she needed three men and four women servants. La Rochfoucauld said that 'in general the English have many more servants than we have, but more than half of them are never seen – kitchen maids, stable-men, maid-servants in large numbers'. Thomas Hanway estimated that the population of London in 1770 was 650,000 and that one in eight was in domestic service.

Servants were generally regarded as members of the household in the eighteenth century. This led to their dressing rather grandly whenever

12 Sunday at the Foundling Hospital, 1872, showing girls in uniform

possible and the woman servant's fashionable appearance and her
persistence in rivalling her mistress in elegance is a recurrent theme in
records of the time, providing a rather odd parallel to the earlier revolt of
the nuns against their sober uniforms and one probably based on the same
reason, a desire to share in the gaieties of the world, to which a drab
attire seemed inimical. In 1725 Daniel Defoe in *Everybody's Business is
Nobody's Business*, which dealt largely with the life of servants, described
an embarrassing experience: 'I was once put very much to Blush, being at
a friend's House and requir'd to salute the Ladies, I kis's the Chamber-
Jade into the bargain, for she was as well dressed as the best. Things of
this kind could be avoided if our Servant Maids were to wear livery as our
Footmen do, or if they were obliged to go in a Dress suitable to their
Station.' A description of modes and manners in a fashionable watering
place as late as 1813 declares that 'as to dress no distinction exists between
mistress and maid, except that one wears a cap'. In 1771 badges or marks
made of coloured braid and worn on the sleeves were suggested for
women servants, it was said at the suggestion of Queen Caroline, so as to
'to distinguish them from citizens' wives and daughters'. According to
Viscount Percival's Diary of 1729 Queen Anne urged a law compelling
women servants to wear 'a sort of shoulder knot of the colour of the footmen's liveries belonging to such a family'; but nothing came of it.
Elizabeth Howard took maid servants to task for their 'Ribbons, Ruffles,
Necklaces, Fans, Hoop-Petticoats and all these superfluities in dress on
which they spend their money'. Lady Mary Wortley Montagu said that
her own sixteen-year-old maid, Fanny, was very like Richardson's richly
dressed Pamela.

Maid servants continued to be grand and to avoid uniforms, and charity
children continued to be forced into uniforms which many of them hated.
Charlotte Bronte's *Jane Eyre* (1847) described the pupils of Lowood, a
school for the daughters of poor clergymen, who were 'uniformly dressed
in brown stuff frocks of quaint fashion, and long holland pinafores', in
which no pride could be taken. The Foundling Hospital of the 1870s was
described later in a book *The Child She Bare, By a Foundling*, which
protested against the Hospital's 'long dresses devoid of cut or shape, which
made the wearer look as though she had no figure at all', at hair shorn
ruthlessly and at the dread of 'service' which hung over the heads of ten-
year-olds.

But times were changing and other women were donning uniforms in
which they took pride as outward signs of the new significance which their
lives were acquiring. The earliest had links with the religious past; it was
that of Quakers, also called the Society of Friends, and it was a uniform in
the strictest sense, being enjoined for all members of the sect with, of
course, separate versions for men and women. It was worn to signify
their complete segregation from the rest of the world, which was a basic
tenet of their beliefs. The sober, dark clothes of the women, with the
distinctive long white collar, close-fitting white cap, and black silk hood,

13 'The Quaker Meeting. An
old print showing the women's
uniforms

remained as changeless for generations as the corresponding sombre clothes and tall hats of the men. Margaret Fell, who in 1669 married George Fox, founder of the Quakers, and who was herself a prominent member of the sect, did not, however, approve of the subdued attire. She thought that women should dress 'in pleasing fashion' and in bright colours, arguing in support of this that outward conformity was the enemy of inward righteousness, which was based on the freedom of the individual. But her theory did not oust the sober Quaker dress. It continued to be worn by many other prominent women Quakers, including the greatest of them all, Elizabeth Fry.

The famous group of eighteenth century learned and cultured ladies known as the Blue Stockings sound like unquestionable contributors to the link between women's progress and distinctions in dress. But they are so only symbolically. Unfortunately for history they did not identify themselves by wearing actual blue stockings and the name so completely associated with them and given to those of their ilk from that time to today came from a man, Benjamin Stillingfleet, a botanist and literary dilettante, who frequented the coteries of intellectual ladies who, about the middle of the century, set out to replace perpetual card-playing by cultivating the art of conversation. His dress is described by James Boswell, who knew him, as 'remarkably grave, and in particular it was observed that he wore blue stockings. Such was the excellence of his conversation . . . that it used to be said, "We can do nothing without the *blue stockings*"; and thus by degrees the title was established.' Another suggestion, that the famous Madame de Polignac wore azure stockings when she visited the London salon of the learned and distinguished Mrs Elizabeth Montagu, is not well authenticated.

The Blue Stockings, though they contributed substantially to the literary as well as the social life of their times, did not establish any main movement or lead any wider crusade; if they had perhaps those blue stockings would have been adopted as an actual uniform.

3 | Women in a man's world

14 Disguised in army uniform, a girl follows her soldier lover. A popular print of 1780

A new world was opened up by a number of remarkable women who in the seventeenth and eighteenth centuries unequivocally invaded the man's world of uniforms and lived out a considerable part of their lives as soldiers and sailors. Proud in their red coats and cocked hats, with swords girded on, or workmanlike in the rougher seaman's gear of the time, they served in the army and navy disguised as men, travelled the world with armies, fought and were captured, ranged the seven seas and asked for no quarter in the most perilous situations. When their stories came to light they created a considerable stir and they add up to a chronicle beside which the achievements of officially recognised servicewomen of our own times seem almost drab.

Admittedly these early women soldiers and sailors were exceptions, but in the context of history they were in many ways pioneers, rebels blazing a trail that, albeit with many windings, was to reach out into the unforeseeable future. They fought in famous battles in crack regiments or on board men o'war and remained undetected for years, in some cases until they chose to reveal themselves, in others until some accident disclosed their secret. How many they were can never be known, for the plain reason that only those whose sex was discovered are on record. Military historian Sir John Fortescue estimates the known cases of women soldiers as about 16, covering some two centuries or more.

Somewhat surprisingly, these women's reasons for turning soldier do not seem usually to have been either a clarion call to serve their country or an early fervour to escape from the trammels of women's conventional life into a wider world. In most cases they were hot-foot on the trail of a husband or lover who had joined the army, old-fashioned girls at heart though Amazons in spirit.

The Scots Greys muster rolls for many years carried the name Trooper Christopher Welsh. Behind this lay the story of Christian Davies, often known as Mother Ross, from the name of a soldier who, she said, had helped her at one stage of her career. Writing of women soldiers, Sir John Fortescue says that 'the fame of all these pales before that of Mrs Ross', and he approaches her with enthusiasm and admiration. She was a redoubtable character, and enjoyed the great advantage that her life story, accredited to Daniel Defoe, was published and appeared in his collected works. His title page announces 'The Life and Adventures of Mrs Christian Davies, commonly called Mother Ross, who in several campaigns under King William and the late Duke of Marlborough, in the quality of a *Foot Soldier* and *Dragoon* gave many signal Proofs of an unparallell'd Courage and personal Bravery. Taken from her own Mouth when a Pensioner of Chelsea Hospital and known to be true by Many who were engaged in those Great Scenes of Action'. That is the gist of it. Christian, daughter of a Dublin brewer and born in 1667, married Richard Welsh who was press-ganged and shipped to the Low Countries as a soldier. She followed him, thus becoming, again in Sir John Fortescue's words, 'our first eminent female soldier . . . not that she was the last'. In 1693, according to Defoe, 'I cut off my hair, and dressed me in a suit of my husband's . . . and putting on the wig and hat I had prepared, I went out and bought me a silver-hilted sword, and some Holland shirts'. As Christopher Welsh she joined a foot regiment and was soon sent abroad. She fought with her regiment at Nimegen, Stevens, Weert and Dortmund and later at Blenheim. When she was wounded at Ramillies her sex was discovered but she remained with the army, started cooking for the troops, then turned sutler – one of the free-lance caterers for the soldiery, whose business it was to acquire food and drink by whatever means they could from the land through which the armies passed. At this she was a great success. Later she and her husband set up in a pub in Dublin, where the fame of the 'female dragoon' brought customers from far and near. She had two more husbands, the last of them being a Sergeant Davies, and with him she completed the full gamut of army life by being made a Chelsea pensioner – technically an out-patient – by Queen Anne and was buried in the Hospital cemetery with full military honours.

15 Christian Davies (Mother Ross)

Some time later a remarkable woman soldier-cum-sailor was Hannah Snell, born in 1723. Abandoned by her husband and unable to pay their debts, she adopted men's clothing and enlisted in a marching regiment under the name James Gray. She deserted, and re-enlisted as a marine. She showed great bravery in naval engagements in the Indies and fought at Pondicherry, where she was wounded and, like Mother Ross, was discovered to be a woman when taken to hospital. She was discharged with a handsome gratuity and her passage paid back to London. As the 'Amazon of the Indies' she was a great success at the Wells-close Theatre, dressed in the uniform of a tar and a marine and singing nautical songs. An engraved portrait of her in uniform was on sale for a few shillings and was in great demand. When her popularity waned she applied to the Duke of Cumberland for a pension and was awarded a shilling a day for life. She opened a public house at Wapping, called it the Widow in Masquerade or The Female Warrior, and had 'pictures of herself in her regimentals on one side of her intended sign and in her Jacket and Trousers on the other'.

Mary Ralphson, known as Trooper Mary, was born in 1698 in the west

16 Hannah Snell, the popular engraving by Phelps

of Scotland and married Ralph Ralphson, a trooper of the 3rd Dragoons. She went to the continent with his regiment, as wives then often did, but the difference in her case was that at the Battle of Dettingen, in 1743, she 'equipped herself in the uniform and accoutrements of a Dragoon who fell wounded by her side, mounted his charger and regained the battle line'. In this guise she continued to serve with her husband in several more engagements of the Duke of Cumberland's army, including Fontenoy in 1745 and Culloden in 1746. Later, on her husband's death, she resumed female life and attire.

In the officers' mess of the Fifth Foot, or Royal Northumberland Fusiliers, there used to hang a crude picture of an old woman in cape and hood, with a basket of wares by her side. Above was a framed picture of a tombstone at St Nicholas Church, Brighton, with an epitaph telling the story of the subject of the picture – Phoebe Hassel, another of the women who served as soldiers. Mary Read has won fame as a woman pirate, but though she was represented in this guise in Capt Charles Johnson's *General History of Pyrates*, she was by choice a soldier, another of the women who served thus disguised as men and only by necessity a pirate. She was, however, brave and resolute, teaming up with another remarkable

17 Mary Read and Anne Bonney

ANN BONNY AND MARY READ, CONVICTED OF PIRACY, NOVEMBER 28, 1720, AT A COURT OF VICE-ADMIRALTY HELD AT ST. JAGO DE LA VEGA IN THE ISLAND OF JAMAICA.

woman pirate, Anne Bonney, who had taken to the high seas in order to join her lover, a pirate captain.

Other cases of women who donned military uniforms and served as soldiers in male guise are less fully documented. In the Register of the church of St Botolph, Aldgate, the entries of baptisms include a 1665 one which records that 'William Clark, a soldier, and Thomasina, his wife, who herself went for a soldier and was billeted at the Three Hammers, in East Smithfields, about seven months, and was afterwards delivered of this child. . . . She had been a soldier by her own confession about five years, and was Drummer to the Company.' A Capt Bodeaux, who was killed at the Battle of the Boyne, was found to be a woman. Mary Dixon served for 16 years in the army, fought at Waterloo and in 1865 was still a strong, powerful old woman. Mrs Dubberley, called by the soldiers of her day Mrs Jubilee, was the wife of a Hussars officer in the Crimean war and seems also to have turned soldier and done some fighting and been present at the charge of the Light Brigade, but she was refused the Crimea medal. A detailed, factual account of the battle of Waterloo by Serjeant-Major Edward Cotton (late 7th Hussars), was published many years later and contains a footnote: 'Many females were found amongst the slain. . . . As is common in the camp, the female followers wore male attire, with nearly as martial a bearing as the soldiers, and some even were mounted and rode astride.'

18 A cantinière of the Crimean war, with military jacket

Vivandières and cantinières, traditional camp followers, both of whom sold victuals to the troops, accompanied armies all over the world throughout the centuries before official provisioning extended beyond bare necessities, which was not till this century. They are often seen in prints wearing military-style jackets and presenting a soldierly appearance.

Other women also went to war before servicewomen and nurses became part of the armed forces. Wives were on the 'married strength' of regiments on active service for centuries. They were distinct from the popular idea of vivandières and camp followers because they carried out many vital and important jobs which were later to become part of service organisation. One climax of their rôle came in the Peninsular War. On that long and bitter campaign many of the men in Wellington's army were accompanied by their wives who, in addition to cooking, washing and mending for the troops, nursed and allotted billets as the army moved from place to place, generally doing as much if not more than future servicewomen. 'They were the pioneers of their sex as far as service with the army was concerned,' says Eileen Bigland in *Britain's Other Army*, her history of the ATS. 'Sick and fevered in the summer heat and cold and wet in the winter snow, fatigued and ill-clothed . . . they trekked gamely back and forth across Europe for six weary years,' unhonoured and unsung. A few died from hardship and many returned as widows. But they fought Napoleon as effectively as many a man, and their work was studied by Florence Nightingale when, nearly half a century later, she was launching her plans for women nurses to go to the Crimea.

19 Molly Pitcher at the battle of Monmouth, 1778, in makeshift uniform jacket

The American Civil War 1861–5 provided a late and startling record of women who served as soldiers in male disguise. 'Of the three hundred and twenty-eight thousand Union soldiers who lie buried in national cemeteries . . . hundreds are those of women obliged by army regulations to fight in disguise,' says a contemporary record. 'Official records of the military authorities show that a large number of women recruits were discovered and compelled to leave the army. A much greater number escaped detection, some of them passing entirely through the campaigns, while others were made known by wounds or on being found lifeless upon the battlefield. The history of the war . . . is full of heroism in which woman is the central figure.'

In addition, the Civil War, calling upon women to take the place of men in a great number of occupations, opening up industry to them, giving them control of money and absorbing them in the community, gave an immense impetus to the movement for their emancipation, anticipating in many respects what was to happen in Europe.

Running away to sea has traditionally been the breakaway boy's most exciting road to adventure and freedom, but history is also dotted with stories of girls or women who took to a life on the ocean wave disguised as sailors, and working as crew members of naval and other ships. Like the women soldiers, they too more often set off in pursuit of a husband or

lover who was afloat than of adventure for its own sake. Sometimes,
however, their motive is unknown, as in the case of Anne Chamberlayne,
who, on 30 June 1690, went on board a fire ship in man's clothing 'and, as a
Second Pallas, chaste and fearless, fought gallantly six hours against the
French, under the command of her brother'. So says the inscription in
Latin on her monument in Chelsea Old Church. She was the daughter of a
London Doctor of Laws. But more true to type was Anne Mills, who
served on the frigate *Maidstone* about 1740, and an episode of 1762 when
'a lusty young heroine, dress'd in a sailor's habit and check shirt . . .
entitled as an able-bodied landsman, was paid the bounty, new rigg'd and
went aboard a tender at Cove, but her sex being soon discovered she was
sent back. Her apologies, and she wanted to get off with her sweetheart,'
according to one report. In 1761 a young woman in man's clothing was
impressed at Plymouth. She was taken to prison, where she confessed that
she was Hannah Whitney and had been a marine in various ships for four
years. In 1772 Mary Lacey, also known as Chandler, submitted a petition
to the Lord of the Admiralty saying that she had in 1750 disguised herself
as a man and served in the fleet till after the war. Then she had worked in
Portsmouth Yard as a shipwright. She claimed – and received – a pension.
In 1781 a seventeen-year-old ordinary seaman, under the name of George
Thompson, joined a ship at Deptford, performing all duties very effi-
ciently, but after a theft, when women's clothes were found in his posses-
sion, he confessed to being a girl, Margaret Thompson, who was following
her sweetheart to Bombay.

The Naval Chronicle of 1807 tells of an old woman brought before the
magistrates for sleeping all night in the street. It was found that, as Tom
Bowling, she had 'served as a boatswain's mate on board a man of war for
upwards of 20 years, and has a pension from Chatham Chest. She had
generally slept this way and dressed like a man.' In 1815 S. Oram, a
Brighton girl, entered herself as a boy apprentice on the *Cicero*, and on
being discovered after eight months, explained that she had fallen in love
with one of the crew. All ended happily; they were married at Plymouth.

A more than ordinary story of disguise and adventure in both army and
navy is that of Mary Anne Talbot (1778–1808). She was the youngest of 16
illegitimate children of the 1st Earl Talbot and her troubles began when a
Capt Essex Bowen of the 82nd Regiment of Foot became her guardian,
seduced her and in 1792, on being posted overseas, made her take to the
uniform of a foot boy and sail to the West Indies with him as a stowaway
under the name John Taylor. She was forced to accompany him back to
Europe and, as a drummer boy, was wounded in Flanders, but managed to
conceal it. Bowen was killed at Valenciennes in July 1793, whereupon she
deserted, took to a sailor's uniform and joined a French frigate, only to
find it was a privateer. She continued to be blown from pillar to post across
the seas, until, back in London, she was treated for grapeshot wounds
received in action long before, and her sex was discovered. She took to
women's clothes and, according to one record, 'amidst her sufferings

20   Anne Mills, with cutlass
and a Frenchman's severed
head. From a print of about
1740

21   Mary Anne Talbot; an
1804 portrait

Mary Anne had the consolation of enjoying a pension of 20 pounds a year from Queen Charlotte'. Not for long, however, because she died in Shropshire in 1818, still only 30 years old. Her story was recorded because for a time she was a servant of Robert Kirby, a London publisher, who included it in his *Wonderful and Scientific Museum* in 1804 and in *The Life and Surprising Adventures of Mary Anne Talbot*, published in 1819.

A close rival to Mary Anne for drama and adventure was the subject of another book, published in 1835 and described as '*The Interesting Life and Wonderful Adventures of that extraordinary woman Anne Jane Thornton, the Female Sailor*, disclosing important secrets, unknown to the public, written by herself.' It tells how she served on the *Belfast*, 'dressed in a red worsted Jacket and duck trousers, like a sailor,' having run off to sea in pursuit of the captain of a ship bound for America, with whom she had fallen in love. He died, and she took to the life of a sailor. Other seafaring women crop up briefly, among them Yorkshire Nan, a servant in Queen Anne's household, said to have made five voyages as a sailor.

As in the army, there were many forerunners of modern Wrens in undisguised women who went to sea with sailor husbands right through history until well into the nineteenth century. In addition to domestic chores many of them went far beyond later women's work in the Senior Service by taking an active part in naval actions as powder monkeys and even firing cannons. There were many of them in Cromwell's navy, and they were expected to pull their weight. 'Wives, real or spurious,' says Evelyn Beauchamp in *The Hidden Navy*, when dealing with sea battles in the Napoleonic wars, 'not only sailed in first rates on combat duty, but did men's work during large-scale engagements, including those major ones with Napoleon's fleet; of the very humble women who applied for medals after the Battle of the Nile as having made up the teams of five necessary to serve each musket-holder, all were aboard first-rates.'

The claims of women to official recognition of their services in the navy at this period, were many. Jane Townsend, who was aboard the *Defence* at Trafalgar, presented 'strong and highly satisfactory certificates of her useful services during the combat'. The *Admiralty Gazette* had directed that all who were present in this action should have a medal 'without restrictions as to sex'. But, as noted in handwriting on the Admiralty medal rolls record, 'upon further consideration this cannot be allowed' – for the odd but revealing reason that 'many women in the Fleet were equally useful'. Several other women applied for the General Service Medal offered in 1847 to all survivors who could prove their presence at any actions in the revolutionary and Napoleonic Wars. Their claim was referred to Queen Victoria, who rejected it.

As regulations in the services tightened wives disappeared and, with closer attention given to hygiene and health, disguise became difficult to maintain, especially in the narrow confines of a ship. The famous naval instruction 'show a leg' was aimed at discovering women stowaways.

To the army belongs the story of the most extraordinary of all women in

uniform and one who fits into no past or future category. Dr James Barry,
described in the Dictionary of National Biography, as 'a woman who
passed through life as a man', strutted the world in high-ranking British
male military uniforms for more than 45 years, rising to hold a rank
equivalent to that of Major-General. That she was a woman was discovered only on her death in 1865. Not till nearly a century later was the
mystery fully investigated, when in 1958 Isobel Rae published her defini-
tive biography, based on an exhaustive study of War Office records, papers
and other material which revealed most, but still not all, of the fantastic
story.

It is still not known who Dr Barry was. She emerges without background as a boy matriculating at Edinburgh University in 1809 as a
medical student under the name James Barry. What is beyond doubt is
that Dr Barry was a brilliant and dedicated doctor, a reformer and pioneer
in hygiene and the control of infection. On applying for admission to the
army medical service, she attested that 'I received a Diploma dated in
1812 as a Doctor of Medicine from the University of Edinburgh'. This
makes her the first woman doctor and first woman MD, beating by a long
lead the pioneers of the later nineteenth century and anticipating by more
than half a century Dr Elizabeth Garrett Anderson's Paris MD of 1869, the
first won by a woman in her own right.

22 Dr James Barry, from a
miniature painted on ivory.
Artist unknown

Barry was appointed to Plymouth, and in December 1815 was gazetted
Assistant Surgeon to the Forces. Next year she was ordered to Capetown,
to the garrison there. She is described as confident and flamboyant and,
says Isobel Rae, 'when on duty Dr Barry appeared wearing a plumed
cocked hat, long spurs and a large sword' – the usual dress of the army
doctor. Three-inch heels aided her diminutive height of only five feet,
and her shoulders were so heavily padded to give width to her tiny figure
that the natives called her the Kapok doctor. She attended balls in a 'coat
of the latest pea-green Hayne, a satin waistcoat, and a pair of tight-fitting
"inexpressibles"'. Lord Albemarle, who knew her at this time, described
her half a century later as 'a person whose eccentricities attracted universal attention', and also said that she was 'the most skilful of surgeons
and the most wayward of men'. 'He was', he added, 'a beardless lad, with
unmistakably Scotch type of countenance – reddish hair, high cheek-
bones. There was a certain effeminacy in his manner which he seemed to
be always trying to overcome.'

She became a colonial medical inspector in 1822 and was a well-known
character in Capetown, riding on a pony in her immaculate uniform,
followed by a retinue of black servants, including a personal one who
became a permanent part of her entourage, as did a small dog, a succession
of such pets always being called Psyche. Professionally she was doing
outstanding work on drugs and poisons and helping to improve the
conditions of lepers.

In November 1827 Dr Barry was promoted to be Staff Surgeon to the
Forces and was appointed successively to Mauritius, Jamaica and St

23   The Corfu sketch of Dr Barry

Helena, where in 1836 she became Principal Medical Officer. Appointed Principal Medical Officer at Trinidad, she led a social life and at Port of Spain was 'a frequent attendant at the Governor's Levees, with a regulation sword as long as himself'. She became Principal Medical Officer of Malta in 1846, then in 1851 was promoted Deputy Inspector of Hospitals at Corfu. Spick and span as ever in her well-tailored uniform, she is shown as she was at this time in a sketch which includes cocked hat, epaulettes, a fly-switch and the inevitable little dog. She treated 500 Cremea wounded, with such success that '400 returned fit for active service . . . in an unusually short period'. She visited the Crimea when on leave, stayed with her friend Lord Raglan, met Florence Nightingale – and snubbed her for her standards of hygiene – which, it was said later, was something only a woman could have achieved!

In 1857 she was posted to Canada, where she provided a spectacle for Montreal with her resplendent sleigh, silver bells jingling and coachman and footman in attendance. In 1858 she became Inspector-General of Hospitals, after 46 years' service in the army, but in 1859 was pronounced by a medical board unfit for further active service. In spite of her protests her career ended. She lived for six years longer, to see her name in Hart's Army List as the senior of Her Majesty's Inspector Generals of Hospitals, a rank equivalent to that of Major-General. She hoped for a knighthood, saying in the Memorial for her restoration: 'I am loath to close a career which impartially may be deemed to have been a useful and faithful one, without some special mark of Her Majesty's gracious favour.' She is said to have ordered a new uniform for the event – but she did not succeed in becoming the first, and only, woman knight. She was by now one of the old brigade, outshone by Florence Nightingale, many of whose reforms she had, in fact, anticipated.

She died on 25 July 1865 in London of an epidemic. Staff Surgeon Major D. R. McKinnon signed the death certificate as that of a male, but when the woman who laid out the body reported that it was that of a woman he put it in writing that the body was 'of a perfect female', who 'had a child when very young'. Dr Barry was, however, buried as a man in Kensal Green Cemetary, described as 'Dr James Barry, Inspector General of HM Army Hospitals, died 25 July c 1865, aged 71 years'.

4 | Florence Nightingale and the start of the modern age

With Florence Nightingale begins not only the real story of the modern woman but also the modern story of women in uniform. Neither has halted at any time since then. Her influence was incalculable and it is sober truth and not sentimentality to say that the lamp that flickered along the four miles of beds which she paced nightly at Scutari in 1854 was to illumine the world. Laying the foundations of trained nursing was only one of her achievements, but in creating the nurse garbed in a uniform which was the prototype of those worn today she took the first great step towards channelling women's energies and abilities into organised work in the community, something of which uniforms were and still often are a symbol.

Some moves had, however, been taken before her, notably by Elizabeth Fry, the great Quakeress. Like Florence Nightingale, she became a legend in her own lifetime but in neither case did the legend wholly accord with the reality. 'Mention of her name', says John Kent, a recent biographer, 'evokes the picture of a quiet, grave, neatly dressed Quakeress matriarchal in quality, seated among the female prisoners in Newgate Gaol, reading to them' – from, of course, the Bible. The dress was right, but the wearer was more dynamic and practical and not very quiet.

Elizabeth Fry was a member of a hereditary and prosperous Quaker family. Born in 1780, she grew up at a time when Quaker tenets were becoming looser, but at 18 she experienced a kind of mystical conversion similar to Florence Nightingale's later 'call', and thenceforth wore strict Quaker dress and followed exact Quaker discipline. In 1800 she married a strict Quaker, Joseph Fry, but did not emerge as an evangelist and reformer until 1816, after the birth of the last of her 10 children. She was accepted as a full minister, free from all restrictions. Her energy, ability and egoism were, like Florence Nightingale's, therefore freed from the conventional restrictions of the time by an inner and over-riding compulsion. Her work, centred upon Newgate prison, combined evangelism with an unremitting campaign to improve the appalling prison conditions of the time. She was instrumental in introducing the prison matron, in charge of women in prisons, a law by Sir Robert Peel.

24   Elizabeth Fry, in Quaker dress and cap

25   (*right*) Florence Nightingale

In 1840 she visited Kaiserswerth, the great humanitarian centre near Dusseldorf, formed in 1833 by Pastor Theodore Fliedner, which included a hospital of 100 beds, run by members of a revived order of deaconesses of Westphalia, whose uniform of blue print gowns and white caps, based on traditional local costume, she described. It was here that Florence Nightingale was later to find a prime source of inspiration, but meantime it led Elizabeth Fry in 1840 to set up the Protestant Sisters of Charity, later called the Institute of Nursing Sisters, which helped to pave the way for Miss Nightingale's reforms. It was followed by St John's House, which in 1848 began to train nurses; Park Village Community, established by Pusey's High Church movement in 1845; the Sisters of Mercy, formed by Priscilla Sellon at Devonport in 1848 and a widespread revival of women's religious orders. These contributed to the future of nursing, but Florence Nightingale was aware of the dangers of nursing control by religious sects and took a much wider view of what was needed.

Her first efforts to train as a nurse in answer to the compulsive 'call' to this work which had come to her in 1837 were, however, made through the ages-old religious nursing sisterhoods, dedicated groups distinguished by special dress. There alone she saw standards which she could respect. Elsewhere nursing, she said, was being done by those 'who were too old, too weak, too drunken, too dirty, too stolid or too bad to be anything else'. In 1847, when in Rome, she contrived to make her first contact with

Roman Catholic nursing sisterhoods there and to study their organisation and training. Two years later she spent a secret and crucial fortnight at Kaiserswerth, to which she returned for three months in 1853. She did not think much of the nursing standards and in 1897 wrote that 'the nursing was nil, and the hygiene terrible', but she greatly admired the spirit of dedication which prevailed. Her attempts to obtain training in nursing continued, and were sought mainly in the Roman Catholic Sisterhoods. In 1852 she wrote to Cardinal Manning: 'What training is there compared to that of the Catholic nun?' She studied Paris institutions and hospitals and in 1853 spent three weeks working with the Sisters of Charity there.

Her Crimea work, developing from this by the circumstances of that misguided war, stemmed from the revelations of W. R. Russell, *The Times* correspondent with the British army at Scutari, whose famous dispatch of 5 October 1854, recorded that in the hospitals there were neither surgeons, dressers, nurses, nor 'the commonest appliances of a workhouse sick ward'. On 12 October he enlarged on this, saying that the French were 'greatly our superiors. Their medical arrangements are extremely good, their surgeons more numerous, and they have also the help of the Sisters of Charity, who have accompanied the expedition in incredible numbers. We have nothing.' On the following day a letter to *The Times* demanded: 'Why have we no Sisters of Charity?' *The Illustrated London News* followed up promptly with a picture of French Sisters of Charity at work in the wards of their hospital at Scutari.

In the immediate clamour that arose came the two famous letters of Florence Nightingale and Sidney Herbert, Secretary at War, which crossed each other, the one offering her services and the other asking her to recruit a staff of nurses for Scutari. Sidney Herbert added, prophetically: 'If this succeeds . . . a prejudice will have been broken through, and a precedent established which will multiply the good to all time.' His proposal that women should go to nurse in the battle zone was startlingly bold.

The party of nurses, formed with incredible speed by Florence Nightingale, consisted of 10 Roman Catholic Sisters from Bermondsey and Norwood; 8 Anglican Sisters from Miss Sellon's establishment; 6 nurses from St John's House, and 14 others from various hospitals.

Before leaving London Miss Nightingale had been formally appointed by the Cabinet Superintendent of the Female Nursing Establishment of the English General Hospitals in Turkey, with all-over control of the nurses, subject to the sanction of the chief medical officer. It was the first time that a woman had been the accredited servant of her country on an official mission and the first time that a uniformed body of women had gone officially to help a war. They went with the Government's approval and at the Government's expense.

On uniforms for the secular nurses Florence Nightingale was insistent, and they had to be made. The uniform, like many later ones for women,

26 A Nightingale nurse at Scutari. By H. J. Townsend

was scarcely worthy of the occasion, but as the party left London on 21 October, only four days after its formation, it is remarkable that uniforms were available at all. The Nightingale nurses wore 'grey tweed wrappers, worsted jackets, with caps and short woollen cloaks, and a frightful scarf of brown holland, embroidered in red with the words "Scutari Hospital"', according to *Memories of the Crimea*, written by Sister Mary Aloysius, one of the outstanding members of Miss Nightingale's band. The scarf was worn over the shoulder and under the arm.

There were various complaints about the uniform. One report says that they did not fit. There was no time for individual measurements; various sizes were made and were issued as they came in, with some dire results. Florence Nightingale also recorded in a letter how one nurse, Mrs Lawfield, protested about the cap which was part of the uniform, saying: 'I came out, Ma'am, prepared to submit to everything, to be put upon in every way. But there are some things, Ma'am one can't submit to. There is the caps, Ma'am, that suits one face, and some that suits another. And if I'd known, Ma'am about the caps, great as was my desire to come out to nurse at Scutari, I wouldn't have come, Ma'am.' One or two of the 'frightful' scarves have survived, and similar ones have featured in women's later military and other uniforms.

The need for the uniform was great, not only for hygienic reasons but also as a protection for the nurses working with the disorderly Scutari army, and it was respected by the soldiery. It was also, like all uniforms, expected to help in inculcating a team spirit into the strangely assorted nurses, but in this it was not wholly successful. 'Ladies' and nurses, Sisters and laywomen, Catholics and Protestants, were not an easy mix, and the religious orders, of course, wore their own habits. There was a big uniformed occasion on the long voyage to the Crimea, when the nurses landed at Malta. A major of militia was put in charge of a shore visit. He marshalled them in military formation, Anglican Sisters in their black habits in front, nurses in grey next and nuns in white in the rear. In this order they marched through the town, thus providing the first-ever parade of women in uniform under military command on army business.

Instructions 'To the Nurses about to join the Army Hospitals in the East' still exist in Florence Nightingale's own writing at the Florence Nightingale Hospital. They are characteristically detailed and unequivical in their strictness and include directions on uniform and other clothing:

An outfit of upper clothing will be provided by Government comprising the following articles

1. Cloak with Hood
1. Derry Wrapper
1. Pair of Indian Rubber Galoshes
6. Check aprons
2. Badges
6. Collars
6. Caps

1. Straw bonnet & cap ⎫ for
3. Print gowns ⎬ Summer
1. Cape or light shawl ⎭ wear

1. Black straw Bonnet & Cap ⎫ for
2. Linsey Woolsey gowns ⎬ Winter
1. Woollen jacket ⎪ wear
1. Wrapper ⎭

1. Box

Regulation I

Outfit & Clothing
Each nurse may take with her as much of her own *under* clothing as her Box will hold in addition to the above.

She is expected to have *in good condition* not less than

1. Dark stuff or cotton gown	4. Nightgowns
2. Flannel Petticoats (coloured Flannel is recommended)	4. Night caps
	3. Pair of Boots or Shoes & all other necessary articles
2. Upper Petticoats	
2. Pair of Stays	1. Brush
6. Shifts	1. Comb
6. Pair of Stockings	1. Small tooth Comb
6. Pocket Handkerchiefs	1. Tooth Brush
	1. Cotton Umbrella

also a Carpet Bag to contain all that is required on the voyage.

27　The famous uniform cape
of the army nurse, here worn by
a Sister of about 1897

After one year's service £2 worth of Regulation clothing will be provided every six months.

II

Nurses dismissed for misconduct will forfeit the whole of their regulation clothing which will be given in charge to the Superintendent.

III

The Nurses are required to appear at all times in the Regulation dress, with the Badge & never to wear flowers or coloured ribbons.

The uniform question clearly loomed large in the Crimea venture, because Florence Nightingale dealt with 'the great dress question' again by sending home to Sidney Herbert a similar set of 'Rules and Regulations for the Nurses attached to the Military Hospitals in the East' with references to complaints and breaches of rules. It was printed and copies were handed out to every candidate for appointment as a Crimea nurse.

The cloak which was part of the uniform is the most interesting item of the outfit. 'The red uniform cape worn by ladies of the Queen Alexandra's Imperial Nursing Service is modelled on that originally introduced by Florence Nightingale for the nurses she took with her to Scutari,' said the *Journal of the R.A.M.C.* in October 1910 'This cape may therefore be regarded as a memorial to the great founder of military nursing.' There may also be a link with the 'night rales' or short capes of early civilian nurses' uniforms.

Miss Nightingale did not herself wear this uniform. A description of 'dear Flo' was given by Miss Mary Stanley, whose arrival with a second group of nurses, unauthorised by Miss Nightingale, created a furore. 'She had on a black merino,' says Miss Stanley, 'trimmed with black velvet, clean linen collar and cuffs, apron, white cap with black handkerchief tied over it'. The collar and cuffs were white, the handkerchief silk. This set a precedent for a distinctive dress for the hospital matron.

Needless to say, the nurses did not all turn out well, and a register of nurses at Scutari at St Thomas's Nurses' Training School contains records like 'dismissed for drunkenness', 'proved utterly unreliable', 'sent home for improper conduct'. Of the original 38 only 16 were really good, 6 of them superb. But their introduction was a historic move. By the end of the war there were 125 of them and they had introduced a new era in hygiene, sanitation, diet and general welfare for the army. For Florence Nightingale it was only the prelude to her life work, but from those crudely uniformed women who toiled and struggled in appalling conditions at Scutari stemmed the whole vast reform of nursing and the largest and probably still the most important of all groups of uniformed women to come, numbering today nearly 350,000 in Britain. There stemmed also a change in public attitudes to nursing and from that to other areas of work for women.

In 1856 Florence Nightingale was given the official appointment of

General Superintendent of the Female Nursing Establishment of the Military Hospitals of the Army. Peace was declared in April and when she returned from Scutari in August the way was clear for her to embark on the enormous Pelion-upon-Ossa of administrative reform of nursing, military and civil, which was totally to absorb her for nearly half a century.

The practical side of her aim of improving nursing had not, however, been forgotten by a public which regarded her as a national heroine, and the sum of £44,000 was subscribed as a tribute to her. 'Her friends knew well that what she would like was the establishment in some form or another of an English Kaiserswerth', says her biographer, Sir Edward Cook, and a Nightingale Fund was set up to enable her to 'establish and control an institute for the training, maintenance and protection of nurses, paid and unpaid'.

It was obvious that Florence Nightingale was not physically capable of setting up and running such a school. She was for many years an invalid, though mentally a demon of energy, and her orbit was, moreover, now the whole welfare of the British army. In 1859 a small committee of the Fund was set up as a kind of action group and in 1860 the Nightingale School was established at St Thomas's Hospital. The matron, Mrs Sarah Wardroper, was superintendent of the new school for 27 years and to her was mainly due its success. She was the first modern matron with full authority over her nurses and, luckily, the perfect exponent of Miss Nightingale's ideals. Florence Nightingale was, however, consulted at every stage of the project and drew up the regulations and programme.

In May 1860 advertisements for nurses appeared. The aim was to find girls of the good domestic servant class, not 'ladies', and 15 were enrolled after exhaustive vetting. On 9 July Mrs Wardroper reported: 'I think the Probationers are a very respectable party.' They were supplied with uniforms by the Fund and Mrs Wardroper duly recorded that all had been given '1 alpaca dress and mantle, 2 print ditto, 3 aprons, 3 collars, 3 caps, 1 bonnet, 1 pair galoshes. I have now a winter dress to provide, but I shall not exceed £4.' – presumably for the entire outfit. The outdoor uniform was a shawl and bonnet and 'a pupil was told off now and again to trim the bonnets'. Underwear was not provided. The print dresses, in the lilac and white stripes still worn today by pupil nurses at St Thomas's, were an advance on Florence Nightingale's earlier thinking; in 1855 she had said in regard to uniform: 'Better I think avoid washing stuffs, they require endless change to look elegant.' A strange comment for a pioneer of hygiene, but no stranger than the fact that Florence Nightingale did not believe in the existence of germs and refused to look into the faithful Dr Sutherland's microscope because she didn't want to see them!

'The nurses wore a brown dress, and their snowy caps and aprons looked like bits of extra light as they moved cheerfully and noiselessly from bed to bed', said a popular-style article in *St James's Magazine* of April 1861, written by Mrs S. C. Hall. The brown was presumably the

28   Florence Nightingale, showing the cap she wore at Scutari. From a bust by Sir John Steell, 1862

winter uniform. She did not add that they also had four more prosaic holland aprons apiece. Sir William Bowman, a friend of Miss Nightingale, said to her: 'Your costumes I particularly liked – I suppose I must not say, admired.'

Florence Nightingale also laid down that 'no crinolines, polonaises, hair-pads &c are to be worn on duty in the hospital'. That the clothing of nurses was regarded by her as highly important had been shown in the previous year, when she produced the book *Notes on Nursing*, designed to give the general public her views on nursing, health and hygiene. It rapidly became a best-seller, running into edition after edition, including a 6d. one for popular consumption, and being translated into several languages. It deserved to be and is still absorbing and relevant today.

On the subject of women's clothing in the sick room, as in other matters, Florence Nightingale was well ahead of her time in her *Notes*. 'The dress of women', she said, 'is daily more and more unfitting them for any "mission" or usefulness at all. It is equally unfitted for all poetic and all domestic purposes. . . . Compelled by her dress, every woman now shuffles or waddles – only a man can cross the floor of a sickroom without shaking it.' Again, she said: 'The fidget of silk and of crinoline, the rattling of stays and of shoes, will do a patient more harm than all the medicines in the world will do him good. . . . Her skirts (and well if they do not throw down some piece of furniture) will at least brush against every article in the room as she moves.' The crinoline came in for special castigation: 'A respectable elderly woman stooping forward, invested in the crinoline, exposes quite as much of her own person to the patient lying in the room as any opera-dancer on the stage.' Uniforms were throwing a spanner into

29   Mrs Wardroper with Nightingale nurses outside St Thomas's, complete with kid gloves

fashion by endeavouring to rationalise that wayward means of self-expression.

But even the uniform of the nurses at the school did not quite come up to the standards of one of the most notable of the early Nightingale probationers, Agnes Elizabeth Jones, whom Florence Nightingale looked upon as her successor but who died young. 'Their dress,' she said, 'a kind of grey stuff, very neat, white aprons and caps, rather too round and coquettish I thought for sisters, but a neat, pretty style of dress, which will, I am sure, be most becoming to Nurse Agnes.' The uniformed nurse, businesslike but also attractive, had arrived and had already moved into the modern context. The matron, as always, dressed differently and Mrs Wardraper is described by Linda Richard, the first nurse to graduate from an American school of nursing: 'A small lady dressed in black. Upon her head was a cap of lace with long flowing strings which . . . hung down her back nearly to the waist. Upon her hands were black kid gloves. During my stay at the hospital I never saw her in any other dress. I think it was her uniform and she was as much at home writing in gloves as the ordinary individual without them.'

Nightingale nurses, backed up by Florence Nightingale's unremitting work to reform nursing, rapidly made their mark and it became apparent that if the school was to achieve its maximum effect it must train nurses to train nurses. In 1867 'ladies' were admitted to be trained for this purpose and to become new-style matrons. Nursing was becoming a respectable profession and in the 'eighties and 'nineties it was said that 'every girl in her teens wants to be a nurse', just as every boy wanted to be a sailor. The ladies paid a guinea a week for their maintenance while training, they were separated from the ordinary probationers and they wore a special dress. They began to appear at other hospitals too.

At Guy's, for instance, there were 'stately alpaca gowns' for them. At the Middlesex they were 'arrayed in a dress of violet hue with a small train, three inches in length, which swept the floor behind them'. The trains, needless to say, became soiled and frayed and the wearers used to turn up the hems. To this the lady superintendent objected: 'I devised this little train,' she said, 'so that when you lean over a bed to attend a patient your ankles will be covered and the students will not be able to see them.' Sisters at this hospital wore deep violet serge dresses and nurses blue cambric or grey gingham. Sometimes nurses were expected to pay for their uniforms and when Miss Burt, newly appointed matron of Guy's, introduced uniform to create a new image for the nurse and required it to be paid for by the nurses, there was a revolt – the staff had just bought new winter dresses of the usual non-uniform style.

But uniforms became general. A paper of the Workhouse Nursing Association said in 1889 that 'we find neat and becommingly (sic) dressed young women in suitable uniform in place of the wretched old creatures who, in pauper dress and black caps, prowled about the beds of our sick poor'. In 1890 the *Queen*, in a report of an exhibition of nurses' uniforms,

30 Nursing becomes respectable. A group at the East Suffolk Hospital, 1867

said: 'Now that nursing has become such a fashionable calling, the interest displayed in the uniforms worn by our nurses is greatly increasing, and was lately exemplified by an exhibition at Charing Cross Hospital of doll nurses organised by the Hospital newspaper.' The report goes on to say that over 200 dolls in different uniforms were shown. 'The Nightingale probationers', it continues, 'wear a lilac and white cotton known as Bengal stripe, a brown holland apron and a spotted net cap. On Sundays and on lecture nights the probationers wear grey linsey gowns. There is no outdoor uniform at St Thomas's.' From the variety of other uniforms it singles out 'the almost universal blue cashmere dresses' of sisters in many hospitals. The diversity continues to this day and to detail it would be an endless task. Uniform was, however, soon universal, and as a vocation nursing had become firmly established. In 1896 Charles Booth said in his mammoth work *Life and Labour of the People of London* that 'in no walk of life has the desire of certain women for independence and usefulness outside their homes found on the whole a more satisfactory expression than in the adoption of the profession of hospital nurses. The census at each decade shows an increase in the number of women so employed. All classes are drawn upon to satisfy the demand. Many are ladies by birth and education.' Class consciousness declined, and in 1910 the lady probationers at Guy's requested to be allowed to wear the same uniforms as the others. Booth refers to the hard conditions, long hours and low pay, but 'in addition to these sums, a uniform consisting of about three cotton dresses with caps and aprons is allowed and about 2s 6d a week for washing'.

The first and greatest army of women in uniform had become a reality, spearheaded by the Nightingale nurses. Their influence was intensified by the extent to which they went out to teach others. 1,907 were trained between 1860 and 1903, and by 1887, the year which Florence Nightingale regarded as her jubilee because the 'call' had come to her in 1837, there were Nightingale nurses as matrons or superintendents in 17 major hospitals. Parties of nurses under Nightingale-trained superintendents had gone to the USA, Canada, Australia, India, Germany and Sweden, all wearing the Nightingale uniform. Four more Nightingale schools had been set up, modelled on the original one and directed by her nurses. Wherever they went they took the uniform she had established for them. Even a record of a visit of the house committee of the General Infirmary of Leeds to Wakefield Lunatic Asylum in 1868 states that the female attendants were 'dressed after the fashion of the Nightingale nurses'.

Florence Nightingale's influence was early felt in the United States of America and the fruits of her experience in the Crimea brought great benefits during the American Civil War. In 1861 she was asked to help in organising hospitals and the care of the sick and wounded there. The employment of female nurses in American military hospitals, with Miss Dorothea Dix as Superintendent of Women Nurses, was largely due to reports of Florence Nightingale's work in the Crimea. As in England, there was opposition to the employment of women nurses in army hospitals, but the innovation was highly successful. In 1865 the secretary of the United States Christian Union wrote to Florence Nightingale: 'Your influence and our indebtedness to you can never be known.'

It was a Nightingale nurse, Alice Fisher who, after introducing reforms into many English hospitals, went to the Blockley Hospital, Philadelphia, 'brought order out of chaos . . . and transformed the nursing care . . . a task requiring superhuman strength and ability'. In the 3,000-bed hospital she set up a Nightingale-style school. Other Nightingale nurses followed her, working to such good effect that a modern American nurse writer has said that 'nursing in the New World was permeated by Florence Nightingale's ideas on nursing'.

The growth of the nursing services attached to the forces also stemmed from Florence Nightingale's Crimea nurses and the first military hospital in Britain to have women nurses on its staff was at Chatham, where wounded men from the Crimea were brought back to be cared for. During the following years women nurses were introduced into other military hospitals. In the Boer War 1,400 army nurses went to South Africa, wearing the grey dresses, white aprons, white triangular veils and red capes that have become famous in their history.

There was also a special uniform designed for nurses in the South African war by Lord Baden-Powell, who wrote in a letter: 'I have had to design a dress for my nurses in my four hospitals. They were coming forward only slowly as candidates till they saw the sketch (so my PMO tells me – but then he is an Irishman!), but now they are sending in applications in stacks – Here is the kit. I can assure you they look very smart!' The scout hat, which he was to make famous later, is introduced in this nurse's uniform, which also shows the Nightingale cape, though it is in dark green and orange.

After the war the formation of Queen Alexandra's Imperial Military Nursing Service was strongly recommended by the Director-General and the QAIMNS came into being in 1902. Queen Alexandra, its first president, took a close interest in it, approving its uniform and being consulted on all suggested changes or adaptation. The grey dresses, white veils and caps and the sisters' scarlet capes were given her approval and are still worn, with, of course, much updating. The Danneborg cross of the Royal Arms of Denmark, her native country, surmounted by the Imperial crown, is also still part of today's uniform.

The district nurse of today in her blue uniform stems from the pioneer activities of William Rathbone in Liverpool, but it was with Florence Nightingale's help that a Nightingale-type school for training nurses for this purpose, was set up there. The first district nursing service began in 1861 in Liverpool and the rest of the country followed suit within a few years. On Queen Victoria's golden and diamond jubilees in 1887 and 1897 sums of £70,000 and £48,000 subscribed by the women of Britain were allocated to the development of district nursing. Poor Law nursing also stemmed from Florence Nightingale, its most notable pioneer being her friend Agnes Jones. This service, which in 1919 came under the Ministry of Health, lasted until the National Health Service Act made it redundant. Another need was met by the introduction of the health visitor, still a key figure in the Health Service. The first health visitors were appointed in 1862 by the Manchester and Salford Ladies' Health Society and in 1892 Buckingham County Council appointed three 'lady missioners' to give home teaching in hygiene and child care, again on the advice of Florence Nightingale.

While nurses' uniforms in all categories have changed and shown variety all through the developments of the profession, the cap has remained a constant cherished feature of almost all of them. It has innumerable forms, but the most famous version, the Sister Dora cap, took its name from a notable nurse, Dorothy Pattison. The daughter of a Yorkshire clergyman and a sister of Mark Pattison, in 1864 she joined an Anglican sisterhood as Sister Dora and became outstanding as a nurse and hospital administrator at the Cottage Hospital, Walsall. She worked there for 14 years, until she died in 1878 when only 46. A stone memorial at Walsall, showing figures taken from life, includes nurses wearing the Sister Dora cap. The cap continued to be worn and was described in the *Nursing Times* in 1909 as 'quite the most becoming yet invented', although it was admitted that its 'strings are not ideal for comfort, but they certainly add to the attractiveness of the cap'. Its eclipse was brought about because its design called for a 'bun' to anchor it.

The Red Cross is not usually linked with Florence Nightingale, but it

31   Sister A. R. R. Innes at the Boer War

32   Lord Baden-Powell's own sketch of the nurse's uniform he designed

too should be. The founder of the most far-reaching of all humanitarian organisations, Jean Henri Dunant, whose experiences at the Battle of Solferino in 1859 led to the establishment of the famous Convention of Geneva said at a meeting held in London in 1872 that, though he was known as the founder of the Red Cross and the Convention, 'it is to an Englishwoman that all the honour of the Convention is due. What inspired me to go to Italy during the war of 1859 was the work of Miss Florence Nightingale in the Crimea.' In 1872 the National Society for Aid to the Sick and Wounded, founded in 1870 under Florence Nightingale's direction, became the Red Cross Society. The most famous of international nursing uniforms therefore also derives from her.

The USA's most famous nurse, Clara Barton, born in Massachusetts in 1821, became known as the Florence Nightingale of America and the Angel of the Battlefield because of her relief work for the troops in the American Civil War, which was comparable in range to what her English counterpart had achieved in the Crimea. She too became a household word throughout her country. Like Florence Nightingale she was a pioneer, organising her own services and supplies with Government help, suffering rigours and privations and even more than her English counterpart working on actual battlefields, alongside field surgeons, continually under fire, with her clothing pierced by bullets and torn by shot. In 1869 she went to Switzerland, because of failing health, and on the outbreak of the Franco-Prussian War offered her services under the auspices of the Red Cross of Geneva. She worked for the establishment of hospitals, organised nursing and relief services, continued her efforts for the civilian population after the war and on returning to America became a representative of the International Red Cross and President of the American National Association of the Red Cross. Like Florence Nightingale she had a profound effect on improving the status of women's work and her lifespan was almost identical with that of Florence, because she too lived to the age of 90.

Women members of the ancient Order of St John, who are represented today in a wide area of nursing and social service, date in their modern guise in Britain from the end of last century, about the same time that the Red Cross was developing. The organisation of Nurses of St John came into being in 1885. But there had been women in the Order, established at the beginning of the twelfth century, long before that, especially in medieval times. They featured notably in Buckland, Somerset, where Henry II presented to the Order an estate for the founding of a commandery and housing the Sisters. There are records of such Sisters under Prioress Fina, who died in 1240, but in February 1539 the Prioress, Katharine Bouchier, surrendered the Priory and the modern story of the women of St John did not start until about 450 years later.

The Order of St John was revived in 1831 in Britain and the St John Ambulance Association in 1877. The first women's nursing corps or guild of St John was formed in Oldham, Lancs in 1885, being quickly followed

33　The original Sister's uniform of the QAIMNS, 1902

34　District nurse of last century

35   Nurses of the Order of St John at the first camp, *c.* 1900

36   Inspection of women of St John *c.* 1925, showing outdoor uniform

by many more. Men first appeared in uniform in 1892 and women in 1894. They wore the housemaid-like uniform of the nurse of the time, which changed very little until about 1920. It consisted of a black dress with stiff white collar and cuffs and slightly puffed sleeves, with the Maltese cross of the Order and the Ambulance Association badge on the

right arm. This dress was covered with a large white bibbed apron with cross-over straps. For outdoor wear a long cloak with a small shoulder cape covered the indoor uniform, the badge again appearing on the right side. A black bonnet was worn on the back of the head and tied under the chin. It was usually of straw, velvet-trimmed and with a white frill round the front. An example of this uniform is on view at the historic London headquarters at St John's Gate, Clerkenwell, the site of the Priory founded in 1140 as the English centre of the Order.

In World War One St John allied itself closely with the Red Cross, the women members wearing a grey nurse-style dress with apron and cap. A coat replaced the cloak. By 1939 women officers wore a black tailored suit, with white shirt and black tie, approximating to today's uniform, which is smart and attractive and accompanied by a distinguishing black felt hat, trimmed with white and caught up at the side with a cockade and badge. The nursing dress is up-to-date, in grey, with the Maltese cross on the bib of the white apron.

Women serve in the 250,000 strong Commonwealth body of unpaid volunteers, 42,000 of whom are in Britain. They work on the 500 ambulances and are part of the body of trained members who attend nearly all State, public, sporting and other events of every kind, as well as demonstrations and theatres. St John's men and women also help in disasters and accidents, assist the aged and handicapped and work in hospitals. They conduct classes in first aid, awarding an average of 5,000 first aid certificates every week. There are 300 centres and 3,500 adult and 2,500 cadet divisions. The whole organisation is financed by private donations; the Queen is Sovereign Head of the Order and Princess Anne is Commandant-in-Chief of the Cadets, whose uniform she wears.

37 Today's nursing uniform of St John (*left*), with former uniform (*right*)

5 Widening horizons

38 The hospital-like uniform of the early Norland nursery nurses, mid-1890s

Other women's uniforms proliferated from the mid-nineteenth century and most of them were part of the social changes of which Florence Nightingale was the first potent instrument. That imperious, almost imperial figure, the British nanny, for instance, whose hierarchy dates from the later nineteenth century, was largely a spin-off from the new respectability and authority which hospital and other types of nursing were achieving. On the broad definition of a substitute mother the nanny had existed for centuries in high-class families and might even be connected with the medieval custom of sending well-born young children to be brought up in other noble households. Until something over a century ago, however, child minders were not clearly distinguished from the rest of the numerous women servants in the rich household. They wore the same kind of not very distinctive clothing and mixed with the rest of the domestic staff. They had no special training. Even the name is recent and its origin is obscure. Mrs Beeton does not use it, but writes of children's nurses. The 1888 Oxford English Dictionary admits only the four-legged goat under the name, but the 1933 Shorter Oxford Dictionary adds 'child's name for a nurse'. Grandmothers were called Nanny in Wales, the Midlands and the North from early times – and, confusingly, are widely so called today. Magdalen King-Hall says in *The Story of the Nursery* that children's nurses were called Nani and Nanna and cites Nan Field, who looked after two generations of the Verney family.

Once established, however, the nannies spread. In late Victorian times, says Jonathan Gathorne Hardy in *The Rise and Fall of the British Nanny*, 'you were barely middle class if you did not have a nursemaid for the children'. He estimates, on the basis of admittedly incomplete census figures and other data, that there were between 250,000 and 500,000 nannies in families of very varied status and wealth. Uniforms for women servants became very important at this time, as their numbers increased, and the adoption of uniforms for nannies which resembled those of nurses was in accordance with the ideas of hygiene and cleanliness brought in by Florence Nightingale as well as with the prestige given by a link with nursing. Nannies in later Victorian times wore caps indoors, with bonnets or straw boaters out of doors. Sometimes the bonnets had long streamers, like those of hospital nurses – and of some smart parlourmaids. Nannies had piqué or cotton dresses for morning, and long skirts of grey alpaca for winter afternoon wear, and of white for summer. These had wide belts and were worn with white shirt blouses, sometimes with stiff collars and cuffs. There were, however, great variations and the nannies' uniforms followed fashion more closely than those of hospital nurses. Thus the Edwardian blouse, the brief waisted jacket with its leg of mutton sleeves and the short skirts of the 1920s all appeared in their uniforms.

What really set the nanny apart from domestic servants was the establishment, from the late nineteenth century, of colleges of training. The initiative in this important move was taken by Mrs Emily J. Ward, an early pioneer of the Froebel system. This stressed the need for trained guidance for the young child and Mrs Ward founded the Norland Institute for this purpose. There were nurseries attached to it and the curriculum covered psychological as well as practical studies in looking after the young. It opened in 1892 at Notting Hill Gate. Uniform was worn from the start and consisted of a long, light coloured dress with a stiff collar and an apron with lace insertion across the bib – some samples still exist. The uniforms were all made in the college and photographs exist of the sewing room with work in progress and an early uniform on a dressmaker's dummy.

Other similar colleges followed the Norland and, like it, still flourish. The Princess Christian College was set up in Manchester in 1901. In 1911 the Wellgarth College was started in London, and more followed in various parts of the country. Each had its distinctive uniform, based on that of a nurse, but more in line with fashion.

The number of 'graduates' produced by the colleges was minute in proportion to the number of nannies in existence, but they set the new style of nannydom. Up to date Norland have trained over 5,000. The other colleges produced considerably fewer, but every nursery-trained nanny followed the college traditions to the utmost limit. 'Nurses', said Norland, 'do not take their meals with the servants' – and nannies everywhere became a race apart. Above all, every nanny wore a uniform usually closely resembling those of the colleges and as strictly adhered to. And whether college-trained or not, she ruled her domain with all the force of the British Raj – and became famous all over the world.

The afternoon parade of the nannies and their charges to the parks was the highlight of their day right up to 1939 and it was a feature of pre-war life in London and other big cities. Hyde Park and Kensington Gardens were the top people's rendezvous, where most of the best London babies were wheeled, but other parks too all had their 'nannies' circles', as exclusive as the high society of the time. Nannies even took the names of their employers. They overflowed everywhere; 'a vast concourse of nannies, thronging, drifting, sitting, rocking, more numerous than the

39   The Princess Christian uniform of 1907

40   A new style for 1929

41 Following fashion more
closely in the 1930s, but also a
link with hospital uniforms

42 Today's nursery nurse in
smart, fashion-right uniform

buffalo on the plains', is Jonathan Gathorne Hardy's description of one
of the chief spectacles of women in uniform in this period.

It is different today. The nanny, or nursery nurse, as the colleges
prefer to call her, has been priced out of existence in many households
where a generation ago she flourished. The *au pair* girl and the baby-
sitter have been invented. But the demand for college-trained nursery
nurses still exceeds the supply and the colleges are flourishing. The
Norland Nursery Training College is the biggest, with 130 students, all
residential. The 21-month course is broadly based and the College is
recognised by the Department of Health and Social Security and the
Department of Education and Science.

Norland uniforms have changed greatly, are modern and fashionable
and come from Harrods, not the sewing room, and are made to measure.
The biscuit-brown dress is smart and a cardigan goes over it for winter.
'Its aim is to be practical, smart, easily laundered and attractive on all
girls', says Miss Betty Medd, Principal of the College. The nap coat is
tailored in a classic style in a warm mid-brown. The bowler-style hat
with the college badge is brown, distinctive and smart.

The Princess Christian College too has a strict uniform, modern in
style, and can accommodate 33 students and 27 residential children in its
nurseries. The uniform is also brown, fashionably styled and they say in
their prospectus that 'This regulation uniform must be worn by every
working nurse after her certificate has been awarded, and may only be
worn by nurses on the College Roll. The uniform must be strictly adhered to and may not be adapted in any way.' They find, however, that
this is not enforceable today, so some relaxation is allowed.

The uniform of the nursery nurse, not always greatly favoured today
either by the wearer or by the private employer, is, however, worn in
new places where the nursery nurse functions. An expanding area of
activity has developed with the growth of nursery schools, day nurseries,
play groups and nurseries for handicapped children. Other posts are as
school matron and nurse on board passenger liners. So though today's
family nanny may wear jeans or a trouser suit, the uniformed British
nursery nurse remains and the tradition survives in a new form.

In retrospect the British parlour-maid, and housemaid, in an unvary-
ing uniform of black dress, crisp white cap and apron, has become a kind
of national institution, symbol of a social stability shaken only by the
upheaval of recent years. In fact, however, her reign in this guise was
surprisingly short in relation to the impact she made. Not till Victorian
times was she established as such an inextricable part of the contemporary
household scene that it is impossible to visualise it without her. In 1901
there were 1,740,000 women domestic servants, and it was the accepted
rule that they lived in. By 1951 there were only 169,000 resident women
servants, employed in only 1·1 per cent of households. Today they are
almost non-existent, even among the upper classes. A *Sunday Times* in-
vestigation into the life-pattern of 14 members of the Conservative

43   Kitchen maids in a country house, *c.* 1874 in uniform

Cabinet of 1974 showed that 7 had only daily help, five had a living-in housekeeper, usually for a country house, and only two, occupying official residences, had a formal staff in the old style.

The uniformed woman servant was also surprisingly late to start her short reign. Mrs Beeton, in her *Book of Household Management* in 1861, find her still something of a newcomer, at least among the wealthy, and says: 'A parlour-maid is kept in many households in place of a male footman. . . . In some households a single man-servant and parlour-maid are both kept, but where there is more than one man-servant she is not needed.' It was still the day of large staffs of servants, even among the middle classes. Mrs Beeton herself had a cook, house-maid and kitchen-maid, plus gardeners, in her house at Pinner. As regards dress, she lays down, 'a parlour-maid is always required to dress nicely . . . her morning attire should be a print gown and simple white cap. . . . In the afternoon her dress should be a simply-cut black one, relieved by white collar, cuffs and cap, and a pretty lace-trimmed bib apron. We know no prettier costume than that of a well and correctly dressed servant of the present day.' The dress was in the style of the time, changing with fashion from the bustle of the 1880s and 1890s to the leg of mutton Edwardian sleeves and then to the narrow skirt and finally to the short skirts of the 1920s. The uniformed maid servant's heyday was over by the 1930s and the Second World War saw her almost complete disappearance, at least in the middle class household.

The parlour-maid was, however, not generally acceptable in the fashionable upper class world until World War One took men servants away to the more urgent area of service for their country. In her life of Lady Randolph Churchill, the former Jennie Jerome, Anita Leslie relates how, when her butler went to the War Office as an NCO, this enterprising American 'engaged two parlour-maids – the first ever seen in Mayfair. She clad these Amazons in Tudor costumes . . . and they were much photographed for the Press. Later on she had the footmen's livery recut for the female form and astounded American visitors record how smart they looked.' Women serving at table were a nine days' wonder.

Mrs Beeton does not detail the uniforms of other women servants, but the illustrations show the same cap and apron, with a plain dress in the style of the time; even the general servant is described as 'dressing herself for the afternoon'. For cooks and kitchen-maids she advises: 'When at your work dress suitably; wear short plain gowns, well-fitting boots, and large aprons with bibs. . . . Servants' working dress, with its neat and becoming cap, is anything but an ugly one . . . and let them remember that, as they allow it is *no* disgrace to be a servant, it cannot be one to dress as such.'

From this time the black and white uniform for the woman servant became general in all classes, but the middle classes gradually led a move over to the coat overall or no uniform at all as class distinctions became invidious. Margaret Powell has recorded in detail the revolt of the domestic servant in the 1920s and 1930s against her conditions and her uniform; 'how I hated it'.

The Penguin-like uniform, however, flourished outside the home. Most famous of all the legions of black-and-white-clad women whose function was to attend upon other people in the early part of this century were the Nippies, the waitresses in Lyons' Corner Houses and in their 200 London teashops and 50 similar restaurants in the provinces. These establishments were part of the large-scale popular catering developed by Lyons, with the first Corner House opened in Coventry Street in 1909 and followed by others in the Strand in 1915, Oxford Street in 1928 and

44   The Victorian parlourmaid in uniform

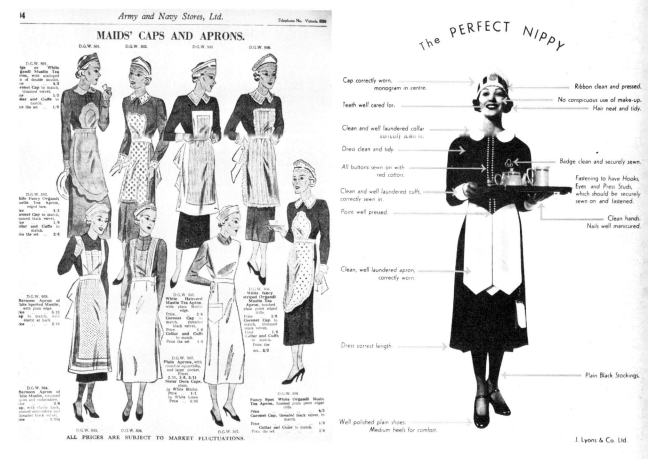

Marble Arch in 1933. The pressure to provide quick and efficient service in these restaurants, some of which accommodated 1,000 people, was met by an army of waitresses whose attentive and 'nippy' service gave them the name. It was officially recognised by the management and on 1 January 1925 a picture of a Nippy, Miss Doreen Vise, first appeared in every London and national newspaper. From them on the Nippy was a national figure, whose uniform was worked out to the last detail and strictly adhered to.

With the outbreak of World War Two the Nippies disappeared. Women were mobilised for war work and the self-service cafeteria became a necessity. After the war it held its popularity, spread and formed the most widespread eating-out pattern for a do-it-yourself era. The large-scale popular restaurant and its stream of crisply uniformed attendant Nippies had become as much a part of history as the once ubiquitous parlourmaid.

Many others of today's uniforms for women had their origins in the latter part of the last century, not all of them limited to women but marking women's entry into new areas of activity and service. One body which was early to put men and women into uniform for shared work was

45 (*left*) Moving with the times; styles of the 1920s

46 (*right*) The perfect Nippy, 1925

47   General Evangeline Booth

48   (*right*) A pioneer party who visited America in 1880, wearing uniform

the Salvation Army, in which, from the start, men and women ranked as equals in every respect. In this the Army was a modern pioneer, carrying out its principles to the extent of having one woman General, Evangeline Booth, who presided over it from 1934 to 1939.

Founded in 1865 by the Rev. William Booth as the East London Christian Mission, it became the Volunteer Army and then, in 1878, got its final name. That members should wear a distinctive uniform was in keeping with the name and the campaigning, crusading spirit which animated them, and in 1878 Catherine Booth, wife of the founder and herself a leading Salvationist, announced its introduction. It was also in line with the times; as the Army points out in its history, there was a passion for uniforms in the second half of the nineteenth century. 'Everybody', they say, 'who did anything special in these days wore clothing which indicated his occupation. . . . From lift boys to funeral undertakers, from policemen, postmen, seamen and dustmen, to the Speaker of the House of Commons . . . men proclaimed their calling in the way they dressed.' It was a time of militarism, stimulated by wars and by martial pride in the great British Empire.

The Salvation Army uniform started with improvised helmets, military caps and home-made badges and hat-bands among the men, in the Army's colours of red, blue and yellow (for the blood of Christ, the fire of the Holy Ghost and purity of life). Women also started with hats, when at the opening of a training school in 1880, Catherine Booth and her daughter Emma, training principal, produced a variety of black straw bonnets of various shapes. A kind of Quaker bonnet was chosen and has remained the basic design for nearly a century – a record in the history of millinery.

A cadet, Annie E. Lockwood, was a milliner and recruited a team to trim the new bonnets with a plaited band of black silk round the brim and black strings to tie under the chin. What became known as the Hallelujah bonnets were sometimes enhanced with a white ruching, and they made their début at the silver wedding celebration of the General and his wife at the People's Hall, Whitechapel on 16 June 1880. The addition of an Army ribbon was made in 1884.

The bonnets had to be cheap, strong and large enough to protect the wearers not only from rain and wind but also from brickbats, tomatoes, eggs and other missiles liable to be thrown at them, especially by the rival Skeleton Army set up by publicans and brewers in protest against the prohibitionist policy of the Salvationists. The bonnets have been updated and kept fashionable, but for 50 years, until 1974, they were made at the Army's clothes factory near King's Cross by Mr William Pope. On his retirement the same traditional methods of construction were continued.

Blue and later red fishermen-type jerseys inscribed with the words Salvation Army in yellow were introduced for both men and women in 1882. The bandsmen began to wear second-hand army uniforms and in 1883 the Army achieved its own uniform. Women at first wore dresses which showed a considerable lack of uniformity and in 1887 they were instructed not to add braid or other trimmings. The suits which have been the women's uniform for many years have changed in accordance with fashion and today are fully contemporary in style, from the neat lines of skirt and jacket to the smart bonnet. The uniform is one of the best-known, but as the Army's membership of nearly 3,000,000 operates in 79 countries there are variations to meet local conditions, customs and climate. Uniforms are fixed by instructions from the Chief of Staff, and are official.

The Church Army's evangelistic movement, which was started in 1882 by William Carlile, later Prebendary Carlile, produced another corps of uniformed women which, it claims, has revived the long-past importance of women in the church and has also provided the first large-scale opening for women workers in the Anglican Church, within which this Army operates. It therefore sees itself as anticipating Women's Lib in its particular sphere.

Church army workers are lay men and women who go out as witnesses of their religious belief and to convert others to their faith. The women, at first called mission sisters, were given some hospital training and approached their religious work by tending the needy and the sick. The first nurse-like uniform was a long black sleeveless cloak, and a black dress with the leg-of-mutton sleeves of the time and a stiff white collar, cuffs and neck bow. A starched white cap tied under the chin was worn

49 The new women's uniform, 1970

50 Church Army sisters, early 1900s, showing indoor and outdoor uniform

51   Uniforms of 1971

indoors and a black straw bonnet for outdoors had black velvet trimming and ties. A large starched white apron was added for nursing.

Developments into wider areas of welfare, social and religious activities were introduced by Marie Carlile, sister of Prebendary Carlile, who joined him for a fortnight in 1880 and stayed for 63 years, lived to be 90 and died only in 1951. Under her, women's activities extended to include housing schemes, holiday homes, visits to prisons and approved schools and help for the homeless, the old and down and outs. Women were commissioned as sisters and captains and had full status as licensed lay sisters within the Church of England. For church services a maroon cassock with a black leather belt was introduced.

As the work moved away from nursing the uniform changed. A black 'schoolgirl' hat was worn for a time, to be replaced by a beret. In the early 'thirties a grey dress in contemporary style was introduced and a military-style grey overcoat with epaulettes and a half-belt was worn for many years. A brimmed felt Trilby hat with a red band was adopted. The initials CA on collars and the insignia of a small sword were the only distinctive emblems of the Army. Dresses were updated with fashion changes.

Some years ago the women's uniform was changed to a grey worsted classic suit, worn with white blouse, or from recent times, a plain pullover. A matching straight coat and a pork-pie felt or velour hat, grey with red band, completes the formal outfit. A hostess cap, originally introduced in 1967 for students, is now available to all. There is a shirt-style day dress and a pinafore dress, each with matching jacket in the contemporary fashion style. Today's uniforms come from Dickins and Jones – but, because of their nature, from the school uniforms department!

A uniform committee has recently been formed, to meet at least twice a year and consider what changes should be made. Uniforms, Church Army women feel, are very important to their work, giving status, opening doors, establishing confidence both in the women themselves and those whom they are helping.

Today the Church Army women form half of the permanent full-time force of over 400 in this country. In the peak period of the 'thirties there were 1,000 and numbers are rising again. With the growth of state-controlled social services, some CA workers have taken state-recognised training, as well as their Diocesan certificate, and work in Youth Clubs, with the Forces and in national welfare services.

The dress of the revived order of deaconesses caused some considerable concern to church dignitaries. In 1872 *Principles and Rules*, published by two archbishops and 18 bishops, suggested that it should be simple and distinctive and the Canterbury Convocation of 1891 confirmed this. The most famous of modern deaconesses, Mrs Isabella Gilmore, sister of William Morris, had firm views on the subject and with the Bishop of Rochester, under whom she worked, she discussed everything from 'the ideals of the order down to the smallest niceties of dress. No detail was considered too trivial.' Her biographer, Janet Grierson, records that the bishop's 'first suggestion was that the deaconesses should wear black, but when Isabella insisted that they had always worn blue, he agreed to this, but emphasised that it must be "a nice blue"'. On caps, Isabella 'treated the bishop to a wide variety of styles, and was only concerned because he was just a bit too serious about the matter'.

In late Victorian times the uniform, worn summer and winter on long walks involved in the work, was formidable. The Head Deaconess wore a blue merino dress with velvet cuffs and lawn cap, and over the dress a long black cloak. The cap was covered with a plain cottage bonnet tied with a bow under the chin, and a long gauze veil. Probationers wore a grey dress and net cap and their outdoor uniform was the same as that of the Head Deaconess, except that the veil was shorter. Isabella also noted that some of the new recruits 'found the uniform embarrassingly conspicuous. Among the clergy too there was some hostility to the women in uniform.'

There were many later changes, including a 1920s uniform closely resembling that of a nurse and a 1930s 'blue cassock, cape and cincture with black or blue cloak or overcoat', suggested by a leading firm of clerical outfitters.

The deaconess's uniform of long navy blue dress and veil, as worn by Isobel Gilmore, was based on the fact that to her the order had a nursing connotation; it was like that of the old-fashioned ward sister. From the 1920s there was a gradual move towards a more clerical outlook and until after World War Two a loose navy blue cassock-like robe, with a leather belt or girdle, was worn over ordinary dress with a long veil. A few deaconesses wore mufti. For a time there was a resistance to abandoning uniform on the grounds that this indicated a lack of commitment, but much stronger was the feeling that the antiquated style of dress, and especially the veil, set up a barrier between the deaconess and those among whom she worked.

For the last 10 years most deaconesses have worn mufti, but some churches have a modern-style uniform, usually a tailored suit. The cassock, navy, black or, more recently, dark red, is worn only when the deaconess is leading public worship, as she does to a growing extent. Sometimes a white alb is worn over the cassock.

For her general work the deaconess usually feels that going out of uniform eases her contacts with those among whom she works as a member of the staff of parish churches; in educational work, which ranges from church schools to youth centres; in work among the aged; in hospitals, colleges and prisons. To the 100 deaconesses at work there were added ten years ago 400 women lay readers, a move which gave an impetus to the move out of uniform and to closer links with the community's general activities.

So far women's uniforms, while multiplying, have all remained in the traditional areas of the religious life and of service – even, in the case of charity children, of servitude. From Victorian times, however, vast new

52 Queen Victoria reviewed her troops at Windsor on 28 September 1837, wearing this uniform

changes began which were to revolutionise the scene and open up whole new areas in the history of uniforms, of costume and of women.

The start of the new era of uniforms, like that of new fashions at the time, came from the top. Royal ladies began to appears officially in versions of military uniforms, and, surprisingly, the young Queen Victoria was a leader in this respect. Writing in 1906 on *Royal Ladies as Soldiers*, A. B. Tucker records that: 'In the early days of her reign, the late Queen used, when reviewing her own troops, to wear a military cap edged with gold lace and a blue cloth coat. On the occasion of the inauguration of the Victoria Cross, 50 years ago,' he continues, 'Her Majesty wore a round hat with a gold band, and on the right side a red and white feather. Her dress consisted of a scarlet bodice made like a military tunic, but open from the throat. Over her shoulders she wore a gold embroidered sash, while a dark blue skirt completed her costume.' It has a considerable likeness to what her great-great granddaughter, Queen Elizabeth II, was to wear at the annual Trooping the Colour ceremony more than a century later.

Queen Victoria did not hold any British honorary colonelships, as future Royal ladies were to do, and 'the uniform she wore was that of no regiment but was merely military in cut'. Some delightful pictures exist of the young Queen elegantly caparisoned in military style, usually mounted on a fine horse. The idea of noble ladies as honorary chiefs of regiments originated, says Mr Tucker, in Germany, where this distinction was conferred on Royal personages and distinguished generals and statesmen, and 'in more recent times has come to be conferred on Royal

53   Queen Victoria reviewing her troops in 1856, in another uniform. Drawing by J. M. Jopling

54 (*left*) The Crown Princess Cecilie and Princess Victoria Louise of Prussia, 1913

55 (*right*) The Duke and Duchess of Connaught in German military uniforms in the 1880s

ladies. These ladies often don the uniform of their corps and ride at the head of their regiments. Queen Victoria was honorary chief of the 1st Dragoons of the Prussian Guard, but she never wore the light blue tunic of the regiment.'

Several princesses of Victoria's family held positions as chiefs of German regiments and wore their uniforms. The German Empress Frederick, a daughter of Queen Victoria, sported the uniform of German regiments, as did her successor, the last German Empress, wife of Kaiser William, who was chief of the Schleswig-Holstein Fusiliers and also of a Circassian regiment; looking particularly attractive 'in the pretty white tunic of the latter, and with a three-cornered hat, her Majesty has often been seen on parade'. Queen Margharita of Italy, the Crown Princess Sophia of Greece and Princess Frederick of Hesse followed suit, as did Russian Royal ladies, both the Dowager Empress and the Empress, a grand-daughter of Queen Victoria. The Crown Princess Marie of Roumania, daughter of the Duke of Saxe-Coburg-Gotha, better known as the Duke of Edinburgh, was honorary colonel of the 4th Roumanian Hussars, and wore their uniform. Queen Alexandra and the Duchess of Connaught both held honorary colonelcies of German regiments, but the Queen did not wear the uniforms concerned.

The feminine regimental uniform usually consisted of the correct male-style tunic with high neck and epaulettes, but with left hand buttoning, and a woman's skirt, riding-style in the case of mounted

56 Women at the universities, as forecast by *The Girl of the Period*, 1869

regiments. The headgear varied from feminine versions of military caps to a German steel helmet, complete with spike and, for the Czarina, with resplendent plume.

In Britain Royal ladies in military uniform disappeared after Victoria, and Queen Elizabeth II wears such a uniform only on one occasion, the annual Trooping the Colour ceremony on her official birthday.

Fashion spread slowly in Victorian times, but could there be a reflection of Victorian Royal ladies in uniform in a curious feature of women's fashions in 1856? All of a sudden masculine fashions began to be imitated by women. 'The hat, pilot coat and ankle jacks adopted by many young ladies occasion them to look very gentlemanlike', says one fashion report of the time. Leather belts, boots with thick military heels and jackets modelled on those of the dragoons all came into fashion.

Although jobs for women were still very limited and the idea of their entering a man's world and wearing the insignia and uniforms of that world was only being born, talk and speculation about the prospect seem to have been widespread. It was not limited to the pioneer women who were, from the mid-nineteenth century, seeking and eventually securing entry to the universities, to medicine, to public life and the distinctive robes that belonged to these spheres. It had spread to the mass of ordinary people. That fascinating contemporary record, the *Girl of the Period Almanac*, which is racy and popular and not at all high-brow, was writing of women in uniform in 1870 in a Below the Stairs context. An item dealing with the proposed Post Office reform took the form of a letter to the editor purporting to come from a man servant 'not fur from Belgrave Sqeeah', and recounting a discussion about careers among his fellow-servants. The scullery maid wants to be a doctor. Then, continues the writer, 'St Valentine's Day being near these gals think of postmen; yes, they'd all on them be postmen! They'd dress hup in the butifullest huniforms, regular milingiary cut, quite the dandy regimental swell with nicker bocker shorts and Hungarian boots! They would flirt with the footmen, get off with men: "You'd steal all the wummen's hand writing from curiosity and all the men's from jellesy!" ' The same publication discusses the idea of women volunteers, with a camp in Mayfair, a Ladies Own Club, and an 'Open' Stock Exchange, with women members. *Punch*, holding up a particularly bright mirror to life in these days, abounds in cartoons dealing with women doing all sorts of hitherto unheard-of jobs in all kinds of uniforms. It anticipated real life by many years and refutes the idea that early moves towards women's emancipation were entirely upper to middle class.

The admission of women to the universities and to university degrees and to full rights of membership was long-fought and not fully realised for nearly 80 years after the efforts started with the opening of Queen's College in Harley Street in 1848, which first put girls on course for university entrance examinations. The actual academic victory was unique in that, revolutionary as it was, it produced no change in long-established academic dress. Here, in contrast to the other spheres they invaded, women accepted without question the established insignia – and they still do. It was a new phase in their uniform story and one which was to be continued in various advances made by women into areas of professional and public life designated by distinctive dress with a long history. For the most part such dress consisted of robes, professional or ceremonial, which were equally suited to both sexes. They have, therefore, no separate history of their own in relation to women. Likewise the complicated endeavours of women to gain entry into the modern church

57 A real-life postwoman of 1862

58 *Punch* anticipated women police in 1853, but saw them overcome by a brawl

as ordained ministers is not an event in the pageant of their uniforms, because here too, they have adopted established robes.

Academic dress was, indeed, so long-established and so highly honoured that it would have been *lèse majesté* to impose fashion or femininity upon it. The scholar's ancient *vestimentum clausum*, its origin, though modified to some extent in the fifteenth and sixteenth centuries, particularly when the hood, originally part of the robe, was detached and elongated, has remained basically unchanged to this day. The half-sleeved gown and square mortar-board are described in 1666 and the tasselled cap in the eighteenth century. Undergraduate gowns also date from the seventeenth century and Charles I ordered the students of Glasgow to wear their gowns in the cathedral, university buildings and in the streets. They are described as red, grey and other colours, but red was early enjoined there and at Aberdeen, Edinburgh and St Andrews – and is still worn by men and women students.

The right of women to wear academic dress was established by the Enabling Act of 1875, which permitted universities to open their doors to women. Dublin did so promptly in 1876 and London followed in 1878, with provincial and Scottish universities following during the remaining years of the century. It is on record that at the first London graduation open to women who had previously passed degree examinations but had not been accorded the actual degrees, some at least of the recipients did not wear their newly-permitted robes. The account comes from Annie E. Ridley's life of Frances Mary Buss, at whose North London Collegiate School many of the staff were London University women. She says that they decided against wearing academic robes for the first formal presentation of 1878 at Burlington House, but next year thought better of this and wrote to the Registrar announcing their intention of doing so. 'There was', comments Miss Ridley, 'no lack of comedy in the situation – consulting a body of staid and learned gentlemen as to whether we should or should not wear the robes to which we were entitled by the University regulations.' Academic gowns were presented to the staff members concerned at, rather oddly, a fancy dress ball given by Miss Buss in honour of the occasion. The hoods has been made by fellow members of the staff: 'the patterns having been taken from that of Sir Philip Magnus, in the intervals of his inspection of the School. Mrs Bryant cut them out, and the pieces left over of the yellow and brown silk are still in the drawer where the thrifty housewives keep their pieces.'

These gowns were worn on subsequent formal school occasions. Mrs Bryant's portrait, in the bright scarlet DSC gown with its amber hood, which she was the first woman to be entitled to wear, hangs in the hall of the new school at Canon's Park.

There is also an account of the conferring of a further degree, that of Doctor of Letters, on three distinguished women, including Mrs Bryant, at Dublin's Trinity College in 1904, when it had also been decided to offer *ad eundem* degrees to women from Oxford and Cambridge who had qualified for BA or MA but were not allowed to receive them from their *Alma Mater*. Fifty women were 'capped', and nearly 90 in the next year. There was some anxiety about gloves and one woman found it peculiar to be taking off her cap in chapel, to which the Provost replied: 'My dear, the whole thing is peculiar.'

The picture of a woman in academic dress which stands out most luminously is, however, earlier than any of these. The occasion was the granting of the Paris University MD in 1869 to Elizabeth Garrett, later Elizabeth Garrett Anderson, the first woman to qualify in medicine in Britain. In face of the refusal of the College of Physicians to admit her to hospitals as a student and of universities to examine her, she qualified in medicine by working as a kind of nurse-extraordinary at the Middlesex Hospital (wearing not the nurse's uniform but 'soft close-fitting dresses in elegant colours, with a linen apron') and then by taking advantage of the loophole discovered in the shape of the Charter of the Society of Apothecaries.

This placed her on the GMC Register in 1865.

Dr Garrett Anderson then proceeded to take the full medical degree of MD in Paris, which had opened its doors to women in 1868 and where she was the first woman to graduate as a doctor in 1869. Her success attracted widespread attention and the Paris correspondent of the *Lancet*, which had previously been strongly opposed to the idea of women doctors, called her graduation 'the event of the day', describing the acclaim given in the crowded faculty hall to the young woman in academic robes who 'presented a most pleasing appearance as their lady confrère'.

This 'golden girl' of the women's movement did not stop short at academic and medical distinctions. On her retirement to Aldeburgh she notched up another 'first'; when her husband died in 1907 during his year of office as Mayor there, the Town Council asked her to serve out the term. So 'once more she made history, at the age of seventy-one, by becoming the first woman Mayor in Britain'. Her daughter Louisa, also an outstanding doctor, described her mother leading her first official procession up the Church Hill. 'A little old woman in a black velvet bonnet with the mayoral chain and robe, an unfurled umbrella in her hand, and wearing stout laced boots, she stepped out bravely to play her part.' She was elected for a second term of office in her own right and was highly successful.

59   Elizabeth Garrett Anderson, MD in 1870

6 | Youth gives a lead

60 Frances Mary Buss

The 'youth explosion' or 'youth revolution' in fashion in the 1960s, when the young seized a lead from the establishment which has never been lost, was anticipated in late Victorian times, when a significant contribution to women's uniforms was made by the development of school uniforms. This new cycle of girls in uniform was not a continuation of the early charity school story, though there was an occasional overlapping of old and new. But perhaps it was not entirely new: Dorothy Margaret Stuart describes school uniforms, complete with school colours, as being worn at the convent school of St Cyr, founded by Louis XIV at the instigation of Madame de Maintenon for the children of needy gentlefolk. Here the girls 'wore blue cloaks, blue gowns, and white lace-trimmed caps leaving part of the hair visible', while 'on each cap was a ribbon bow of the colour of the division of the school to which the wearer belonged, blue for the seniors, green for those next in age, yellow for those younger still, and red for the youngest of all'. The school continued till the French Revolution. Felicia Lamb sees Quaker Schools for girls as significant: 'Their plain, hard-wearing costumes, economic levellers among the Society of Friends were a prerunner of school uniform.'

What happened from about the 1870s was, however, different. The mid-Victorian upper- and middle-class girl, among whom school uniforms began, was brought out of her version of contemporary, restricting fashion by the introduction of active games and gymnastics into the school curriculum. This called for drastic dress reform and the pioneers of girls' higher education were also pioneers in bringing comfort and ease into fashion for the first time in history. The first and foremost of them all, Frances Mary Buss, who set up the North London Collegiate School for Ladies (later changed to Girls) in 1850 and made it 'the first public day school for girls, the model of the present High School', took a leading part in promoting active games and physical exercise as well as in improving and developing classroom teaching. She campaigned against tight clothes, especially the fashionable heavy boned and tightly laced corsets, advocating clothes that hung freely from the shoulders. 'Miss Buss,' says her biographer and friend, Annie E. Ridley, 'would have liked a school uniform which she would have made graceful as well as rational; but, except in the gymnasium, she never attained this desire, and had to content herself with at school advising and at Myra [the boarding house which she supervised] compelling the most needful reforms. . . . She was a reformer and to her clothing needed reform – but it was the hardest thing of all to rationalise.'

When the school was re-built in 1872 it included a gymnasium, 'a splendid room 100 feet long, and about 40 feet high', where every class had a lesson twice a week, plus short daily drill, and where there was also a special afternoon class and another for remedial exercises recommended by the school doctor. An American system of musical gymnastics was introduced, with a trained teacher in charge, and an 1882 picture shows one main piece of equipment, the giant stride, with girls wearing the beginnings of school uniform. A demonstration of drill was given before Queen Victoria at the Health Exhibition. A pupil who left the school in 1890 recalled that she had been 'very proud of my blue jersey and skirt and wide red sash round my middle', though another declared that 'our energies were sapped by the weight and cumbrousness of our clothes. On drill days we had the added burden of a voluminous pale blue sash swathed round the waist to give some semblance of uniform.'

In 1890 there was a big occasion when the games captain, Ethelda Budgett-Meakin, who sounds like an invention of Sir John Betjeman, 'persuaded Miss Buss to introduce Olympic games and competitions. At that date outdoor sports for women were an unheard-of event.' A field at Epping was hired, but owing to bad weather the event had to take place in the town hall. For the games 'each girl wore a light coloured skirt reaching only to the knee, a white blouse loosely belted at the waist, a cap either

61 The Giant Stride, 1882

62　The 1902 hockey team

63　Dorothea Beale

blue striped (art) or red striped (science)'. Reports of the second and third such games, recorded in the school magazine, describe how 'the gymnasium was full of girls, some in the gymnasium costume, others in short bright-coloured skirts and white blouses, but all wearing scarlet-and-white or red-and-white caps. The effect was very pretty.' Next year everyone wore short skirts and white blouses, with yellow and blue sashes, 'according as they were partisans of the new or old universities'. It was a revolution in dress.

Minutes of monitors' and prefects' meetings of the last decade of last century record how, under Mrs Sophie Bryant, Miss Buss's successor, uniforms developed. At first they were only for gymnastics, but by 1899 Mrs Bryant was recommending that uniform be worn all morning. Regulation ties, belts and shoes were specified in 1901. A hockey team photograph of 1902 shows everything correct, with shirt blouses, striped ties, calf-length skirts and schoolboy caps.

Dorothea Beale, co-pioneer with Miss Buss of girls' education, disliked both uniforms and sport. The former was due to an unhappy year teaching at Casterton, the school for clergymen's daughters which had achieved unwelcome fame as the original of Lowood in *Jane Eyre*. Though it had improved greatly by Miss Beale's day, 'the pupils wore a hideous uniform which seemed to her to emphasise the petty restrictions which encompassed them, and which gave her a permanent horror of regimentation and a dislike of school uniform', says Josephine Kamm.

The fact that she had visited Kaiserswerth in 1856 and stayed with the Fliedners did not apparently alter this view. Details of the dress at Cheltenham Ladies' College, where Miss Beale began her notable career as principal in 1857, are given by F. Cicely Steadman in her book, *In the*

Days of Miss Beale. She states that there was no uniform except on Sundays, when brown was worn in winter and white in summer. The only rules were that hair had to be tied back or pleated in the morning, and heels had to be low, 'but we all knew that red must be avoided because Miss Beale did not like it'.

Paradoxically, the opponent of uniforms introduced the most distinctive and longest-lasting of all items of schoolgirls' uniform — the hard straw boater. 'In summer, for College and ordinary occasions,' says Miss Steadman, 'we wore coarse white straw hats with house colours, exactly like a boy's "straw", and these were called boaters because in high society they were considered correct for punting on the Thames. In winter and for best we wore whatever our mothers chose.' At first bustles and tight lacing prevailed and girls did many exercises in 'a sort of armour that clasped us tightly in all sorts of agonising places', but Swedish exercises were introduced and within a year 'we were wearing washing blouses and skirts in school, instead of frocks with fitting bodices'. Smart pupils wore high starched collars like their brothers, but had lower ones for games days. Women's uniforms were still copying men. The first complete Cheltenham uniform was introduced by Miss Beale's successor, Miss L. A. Faithfull, and consisted of a navy skirt and white blouse.

Up north, in St Andrews, St Leonards School blazed a trail for uniforms as well as for new-style education for girls. Established in 1877 on the lines of boys' public schools, it was the model for many future girls' schools in England. Its ruling spirit at the outset was Miss, later Dame, Louisa Lumsden, the most dynamic of the first five women students whose careers at Hitchin under Miss Emily Davies had been the first breakthrough for women into Cambridge and the nucleus from which sprang Girton College in 1873. Louisa was teaching at Cheltenham under Miss Beale when she was urged to accept the St Leonards post. Uniform came to the fore of her planning for the school. She saw it as a means of fostering a corporate spirit as well as providing freedom for the games to which she gave close attention. 'Dress', she said long afterwards in her book of reminiscences, *Yellow Leaves*, 'may seem a trifling thing, but even from childish days it had worried me. I wanted to be free to run, jump and climb trees.' With her, too, uniform was a kind of dress reform. Her first choice was, she said, adapted from one worn at a Belgian school and it consisted of a blue knee-length belted tunic, with knickerbockers or trousers underneath. These could be of any length, as if in anticipation of the trousers suits of nearly a century later. From being worn only for gymnastics and games, this outfit, which proved very popular, soon spread to general wear, but for this purpose was standardised into a tunic with shorter knickerbockers, both of navy serge. For outdoors tam o'shanters were worn from 1887, usually in the house colours, and a dark blue cloak, lined with red, was copied from a style worn by peasant women of the Pas de Calais. The uniform, in retrospect, proved to be ahead of fashion. One recollection of early days says in 1927: 'In 1877 the girls in

64 The lacrosse team of St Leonards, 1888, wearing the early uniform, with tam o'shanters

65 (*right*) The uniform of 1904–5

this school actually wore, in their own grounds, a dress assimilating in essentials to the ordinary dress of today.' Uniform was developed largely under Miss Frances Dove, who had succeeded Miss Lumsden in 1882, and who, like her, had taught at Cheltenham.

Roedean, founded in 1885, was from the first prominent in sport. An early photograph shows the uniform of long braid-trimmed skirts, with sailor blouses, which came in about the turn of the century. Later a professional dress designer, working with the head mistress, Miss Dorothy Lawrence, produced a djibbah, which she said was inspired by the dress of North African tribesmen! 'It was much liked by the girls when first displayed by the Founder's niece, Doffie, though parents received it less kindly', says the school historian, Dorothy E. de Zouche. 'It appeared in school scenes in *Punch* when the well-known artist, L. Raven Hill, had a daughter at Roedean.' An enveloping cloak was also worn. Sunday dress, as at many other schools, was white serge coat and skirt, 'no more popular than practical'.

The djibbah, mentioned by many other schools, gave way to the orthodox gym tunic, which was in existence by 1890, when it is seen worn with the leg-of-mutton sleeved blouse of the time. It remained in wide favour for more than half a century, is still worn today and has also merged into the pinafore dress of the 1970s fashion scene. Wycombe Abbey took its cue in this respect from St Leonards, just as it took its first head mistress, Miss Jane Dove, plus four mistresses and four girls as heads of houses in a kind of colonisation process. One of the original pupils, Winifred Peck, records that in a régime which included cold baths, fresh air and games galore, 'part of the fun came from the games dress –

66 (*above left*) The straw boater, worn by a sketching party, 1899 at St Leonards

67 (*above right*) Gym tunic of 1890, the earliest on record

68 (*left*) The sailor suit as girls' school uniform about 1900 at Roedean

short tunics and baggy bloomers, with tam o'shanters which always fell off'. For ordinary wear there was no uniform, 'or rather there was none as regards our outward appearance. Our underclothes, however, were standardised well and truly, and how we endured them I cannot imagine.'

Other schools followed similar patterns. Loose serge dresses or tunics, shirt blouses, school colours worn on hat bands and ties were general. Sara Burstall, head mistress of the Manchester High School for Girls, reviewed the school uniform question in her book *English High Schools for Girls* in 1907. She says: 'Dress with girls has an important bearing on health, and dress reform was advocated and encouraged more than 30 years ago by the pioneer women in education. The growth of games and gymnastics has done much, very much, for reform. Girls brought up to vigorous open-air exercise will not endure excessively tight, heavy, unhygienic clothing. . . . School authorities generally make sumptuary rules which the homes on the whole loyally follow. . . . Tact is needed, lest the mother should feel her authority and taste interfered with, and sometimes there are difficulties. . . . Indeed the girls' schools can do something to influence opinion about dress.'

Christ's Hospital, flourishing today as a progressive girls' public school, offering a broadly based curriculum to its 250 boarders, maintains the continuous tradition of uniform established in 1523. The original dress, with only minor changes, was actually worn until 1873, when the newly appointed principal, Mrs Susan Lyster, decided that 'a neat useful dress, uniform but more assimilated to that of today, be introduced, but that the previous colour and material should continue to be used'. A dress of this time, 'a plain blue serge with a small upright white collar', made in the style of the day, still exists in the school's dress department, beautifully made as befits a school with a long tradition of fine sewing. For the girls it was liberation: 'No longer need they labour with miniature flat-irons at the unending laundering of the deep starched collars which used to fret and chafe their necks', says Frances W. Page, MA, PhD, a distinguished member of the staff who wrote the school's history in 1953.

But some cherished relics from the past survive. In 1899 the then head mistress, Miss Margaret E. Robertson, introduced a distinction between junior and senior girls in the form of black aprons for seniors and white for the younger pupils. The black ones are still worn by fifth formers selected as potential monitresses. Monitresses wear green aprons of similar style – in each case during meals and when doing work that calls for protection. Until 1943 all girls had to be 'covered' not only in church but also when dining in their own hall, wearing little round caps for this purpose. But, apart from that, the school has proceeded on modern lines in all that concerns its uniforms and its work.

Those Roedean girls with their sailor blouses, were illustrating another curious vogue in uniforms for the young which prevailed for more than half a century and even today has left some traces. This was the wearing of sailor suits. Small boys had set the fashion when, about 1860, sailor collars appeared on their coats, to be followed within a few years by sailor suits, with bell-bottom trousers, shown in a photograph of 1882, and also, about 1880, by fishermen's jerseys. Girls joined in and for many years were sailors from the waist upwards, wearing navy serge dresses and jackets with sailor collars trimmed with rows of white cotton braid. 'By the Edwardian decade,' says Doris Langley Moore, 'when a series of photographs of the Royal families of Europe was published in the *Girls' Own Paper*, there was scarcely a young prince or princess who did not appears to be going to sea'. With these outfits straw boaters were frequently worn before they became almost standard school uniform, and other types of sailors' hats and caps also appeared on youthful heads.

The traditional dress of Scottish fishwives, with its distinctive striped petticoat and kilted or looped-up skirt, was also adapted as a young girl's fashion which lasted from Victorian times until the second decade of this century. The original version is notable as the last occupational costume for women to survive in its full 'uniform' authenticity to today. Almost unchanged for about 200 years, it is seen in its real-life form in a series of about 40 calotypes created by R. Adamson and D. O. Hill in June 1845 at Newhaven and Calton Hill, Edinburgh, with three families of fishwives seen at work. The distinctive costume, to all intents and purposes a uniform, was based on the eighteenth century attire of house and field workers, which by that time was becoming formalised.

Kay's *Portraits*, about 1796, gives a full description of the fishwife's dress as it was worn then, and for long afterwards. 'A cap of cotton or linen, surmounted by a stout napkin tied below the chin, comprises the investiture of the head. . . . A sort of woollen pea-jacket, of vast amplitude of skirt, conceals the upper part of the person, relieved at the throat by a liberal display of handkerchief. The wider part of the figure is invested with a voluminous quantity of petticoats, of substantial material and gaudy colour, generally yellow with stripes, so made as to admit of a very free inspection of the ankles, and worn in such immense numbers, that the mere mention of them would be enough to make a fine lady faint. One half of these ample garments is festooned up over the haunches, puffing out the figure in an unusual and uncouth manner. White worsted stockings and stout shoes complete the picture.'

Until well into this century the dark working version was still worn by fishwives selling their wares from door to door in Edinburgh and elsewhere in the East of Scotland. The gala dress is still treasured and appears at an annual Fisherman's walk in Musselburgh, where the special garments that constitute it are handed on devotedly from one generation to another. The full costume is also worn by the Newhaven Fishwives' Choir, composed of local women who are descended from working fishwives and who thereby preserve the local costume tradition intact, without any 'folksy' variations.

The costume today consists of a dress with full mid-calf skirt, gaily striped for gala occasions, with striped petticoats revealed by the kilting,

69   Newhaven fishwives of the 1840s in traditional dress

70 The same dress worn in 1973 by the Newhaven Fishwives Choir

71 Princess Helena, daughter of Queen Victoria, in Highland dress in the mid-1850s

a white apron, a pea jacket or shawl and on the head a cap, 'mutch' or small shawl. White stockings for Newhaven and black for Musselburgh are a continuing distinction. The schoolgirl version took over the striped petticoat, red and white, as often with fishwives, and a navy serge tunic, looped up and often with a sailor collar, to ensure the full nautical air for this uniform with a history of its own.

Highland dress had a similar vogue among the young of both sexes in the last century and thereby provided another footnote to the uniform story of the time. 'As soon as little people leave off their suits,' said *The Englishwomen's Domestic Magazine* in the mid-nineteenth century, 'they should be put into Highland costumes, which are not only the prettiest dresses for boys and girls, but also the most healthy.' The fashion was even more prevalent in America than in Scotland and England, and it was much favoured for small boys for many years to come. It too was adopted by young members of the Royal family, both girls and boys.

Even more than previous cases of the 'youth explosion' of girls into uniforms, the Girl Guide movement started as a case of 'girls will be boys', because it grew directly out of the Boy Scout movement. This originated in the handbook *Aids to Scouting*, published by the War Office in 1899 for army officers and men. Written by Col. R. S. S. Baden-Powell, it set out his novel idea for developing responsibility and independent thinking among servicemen. The adaptation of it to boys was, however, rather unexpectedly, due to a woman, Miss Charlotte Mason, Principal of an Ambleside training college for governesses, who was so impressed with its possibilities as a means of developing initiative among children that she included it among recommended reading for her students. This got back to Baden-Powell, who thereupon wrote his

Scouting for Boys, out of which grew the Scout movement with its uniform of wideawake hat, khaki shirt, shorts and coloured neckerchief, to some degree based on army tropical dress in India and South Africa, where he served. Jerseys were also worn.

At this point girls latched on to the idea. Baden-Powell was inundated with letters from them begging to be allowed to be 'Boy Scouts'. His discouraged them, but hundreds acquired Scout badges by the simple expedient of giving only the initials of their names when applying for them. At the first Scout Rally at Crystal Palace in September 1909, the 11,000 boys who turned up for the march past were joined by a rearguard of girls dressed in Scout jerseys, neckerchiefs and hats and carrying Scout poles – Boy Scouts in all but their long hair and calf-length skirts. 6,000 girls had by this time registered as 'Boy Scouts'. They proved a problem for Baden-Powell, who, while welcoming their enterprise, realised that his Boy Scouts would resent this female invasion of their chosen province. He therefore evolved *The Scheme for Girl Guides*, which appeared promptly in the *Scout Headquarters Gazette* in November 1909. The name came from a regiment of guides in India, noted for their resourcefulness and ability to tackle any kind of job that came their way. He entrusted the formation of the Girl Guides to his sister Agnes and by 1910 there were 8,000 Girl Guides in the United Kingdom, with their own one-room office at Scout headquarters.

The first uniform, laid down in the *Scheme for Guides*, was described in detail as 'Jersey of company colour, Neckerchief of company colour. Skirt, knickers, stockings dark blue. Cap red biretta, or in summer large straw hat. Haversack, cooking billy, lanyard and knife, walking stick or light staff. Cape hooked up at the back. Shoulder knot of the group colour on left shoulder. . . . Badges much the same as Boy Scouts.' For officers there was to be 'ordinary country walking dress, with biretta of dark blue, white shoulder knot, walking stick and whistle on lanyard'.

The Girl Scouts had, however, in many cases designed their own uniforms and some groups continued to wear them for several years. One, on view at today's headquarters, a large building in Buckingham Palace Road, has a Scout hat turned up at one side with a big bunch of cock's feathers, like the South African war nurse's hat, a style that was very popular in early days. So were white haversacks with huge red crosses on them. Green and khaki were worn as well as blue for uniforms, and tam o'shanters were stuffed with paper to make them stand up stiffly on the head – making uniforms fashionable has been a recurrent feminine aim. The straw hats were the 'boaters' of school and general fashion at this time.

Though school uniforms were accepted, the idea of girls marching, drilling and taking part in strenuous outdoor activities in the manner of boys, not to mention going to camp (as early as 1910), sometimes roused jibes and cat-calls when the girls paraded in their uniforms. World War One, however, put an end to the idea of the sheltered woman, and soon after it ex-army sergeant majors were organising marching, drilling and heel-clicking and were helping with camps. Guides were little soldiers, keeping sentry-go at camps, and uniforms were brisk and businesslike.

As the war receded, interests became wider, and the movement spread rapidly. Officers became Guiders, to lessen the militarism: older Guides became Senior Guides, later re-named Rangers. As early as 1914 little sisters had also wanted to join and a junior branch was formed. It started with the disastrous name 'Rosebuds', but in 1915 this was changed to Brownies, an inspiration of Lord Baden-Powell, based on the Brownies in Mrs Ewing's story of Tommy and Betty and the Brownies, who did good deeds in the home without ever being seen. A brown overall dress and an alternative jersey and kilted skirt were the chosen uniform, and while the Guides' uniform has changed repeatedly, Brownies still remain very similarly clad today, though the jersey and skirt were abolished in 1969. The brown cotton dress introduced in 1939 has changed little, but there have been many changes in headgear, from straw 'pudding basins' to today's neat berets. In 1967 the youngsters were re-named Brownie Guides.

In 1916 cadets were introduced into schools and colleges as a kind of girls' version of the army-style cadets at boys' schools. In 1920 Sea Guides were introduced, largely as the result of an infiltration of ex-WRNS women, dismissed abruptly from the Navy at the end of the War. In 1922

72   The 1st Kidderminster Girl Guides, 1909

Dame Katherine Furse, wartime head of the WRNS, was drawn into the Guides by Lady Baden-Powell as Assistant Chief Commissioner to her and also head of the Sea Guides. The uniform of the latter since then has always been a cross between that of the WRNS and that of the Guides. In 1927 the name was changed to Sea Rangers. In 1943 Air Rangers were introduced, and the two groups enjoy recognition by the Royal Navy and the Royal Air Force.

Until the mid 'thirties one uniform was worn by Guides on all occasions, from ceremonial events to camping, but about 1936 a short-sleeved camp dress, stitched cotton hat and ankle socks were introduced, to be followed by shorts and a cellular blouse, also for camps. Sea Rangers were allowed to wear slacks or shorts with shirts for boating. Now jeans, slacks or shorts are allowed at camp and as working dress for everyone, with a casual uniform blouse.

After World War Two a navy battle-dress top and skirt were adopted for Rangers and Guiders, with distinguishing shirts – grey for Land Rangers, white for Sea groups and Air Force blue for the air-minded. Guides wore berets, and uniform moved nearer to contemporary young casuals. In 1959 Guiders and Rangers were updated with a boxy suit which received the accolade of approval from Norman Hartnell, Royal dressmaker and himself the designer of many women's uniforms.

In 1964 the air hostess cap replaced the beret for Guides, and the rise of teenage fashions at this time brushed off on the Guides' uniforms, bringing in an over-blouse with a V-neck and collar. Guiders in 1966 shed stiff collars and ties and wore a mini-care poplin blouse in a blue and white check, and air hostess cap. In 1967 Rangers were re-kitted in aquamarine open-necked shirts, navy skirts and aquamarine-piped caps.

The Girl Guide movement is unique in the extent to which Royal

75 Uniform of 1967, still worn. (*left to right*) Guider, Brownie, Girl Guide, Ranger Guide

ladies have been involved in it from early days and have worn its uniforms. The late Princess Royal was President of the Girl Guides Association from 1920 until her death in 1965. In 1937 Princess Elizabeth was enrolled as a Guide in a Buckingham Palace company and Princess Margaret, now President, as a Brownie in a Palace pack. During the War they were members of a Guide Company at Windsor and later both became Sea Rangers. In 1959 the Palace Brownies were re-formed, with Princess Anne as a member and in 1961 she became a Guide in the 1st Buckingham Palace Company.

With a membership of $6\frac{3}{4}$ millions in 91 countries, all linked by prescribed uniforms as well as by shared aims and activities, the World Association of Girl Guides and Girl Scouts, formed in 1928, is probably the biggest female organisation in the world. It has no barriers of creed, race, class or nationality and it covers all ages, from seven-year-olds to octogenarians: The World chief Guide, Olave, Lady Baden-Powell was born in 1889. In Britain the Girl Guides Association has a membership of about 772,000, including 64,000 adult leaders. Uniforms, insignia and badges are so numerous that details of them occupy eight pages of an official manual.

7 | Determined to serve

Rather unexpectedly, the Votes for Women campaign, which brought organised women so violently into the limelight in the years before 1914, did not contribute much directly to the story of women in uniform, mainly because the participants were anxious to show that they were the representatives of all ordinary women, not a special group. For the vast demonstrations they staged they sometimes adopted white dresses as symbols of 'injured innocence' and across their shoulders they often wore Nightingale-style bands or sashes in the red, green and white colours of the non-militant National Union of Women's Suffrage Societies (NUWSS) the purple, green and white of the militant Women's Social and Political Union (WSPU) or the green and gold of the Women's Freedom League (WFL). Blouses in the colours of these groups were also worn. In 1908 banners and flags were the distinguishing marks at the great rally organised by the WSPU in Hyde Park, when a quarter of a million women were brought by 30 special trains from all parts of the country to the largest demonstration ever held in Britain, with speeches delivered from 20 platforms. The NUWSS also organised a mammoth procession in this year, with banners emblazoned with the figures of Joan of Arc and Queen Elizabeth and with prominent women parading in their professional or occupational uniforms, among them nurses, doctors and other graduates in hoods and gowns.

The next stage in women's uniforms, however, looked back once more to the 'angel of mercy' tradition, though it rapidly took off in other directions, leading to a new concept of women in uniform. The practical start of women as a recognised and uniformed part of the armed services stemmed from 1907, when the still active and flourishing FANY (First Aid Nursing Yeomanry) was formed. It sprang neither from the general emancipation movement nor from the 'Votes for Women' campaigners, but from a man, a sergeant major named Baker who had been wounded in Kitchener's Sudan expedition of 1898. He saw that the ambulance service failed to provide any means of bringing immediate first aid to the wounded on the battlefield and felt that this could be done most effectively by a band of mounted nurses who would ride out from the field hospitals

76   The first women's military
uniform. FANY, 1909

to the actual scenes of action. Captain Baker, as he became known, was
the leading spirit in the formation of such a force, each member of which,
he planned, would be trained in first aid and also in cavalry movements,
signalling and camp work, so as to be able to ride with the skirmishing
parties. Therefore the title, though service as a mounted force ended in
1915 and nursing later went by the board. By September 1907 press
advertisements had produced a troop of young women volunteers who
saw in this scheme an exciting and worthwhile outlet for pent-up energies.
As the movement was voluntary and unpaid and as members had to be
expert horsewomen, with their own mounts, the first FANY's came mostly
from the upper classes and the group had a 'county' air. They undertook
first aid courses and were given facilities for riding practice at the Surrey
Yeomanry headquarters. In May 1908 they were invited as a troop to the
Royal Naval and Military Tournament by Col. F. C. Ricardo of the
Grenadier Guards and soon afterwards they took part in a riding competition at Crystal Palace. Next they were invited to drill at the Albany
Barracks, where a major of the Blues offered to be their riding master and
other officers joined in. They were even allowed to ride the Blues' own
black horses; in those days War Office protocol was much less strict than
now.

The corps began to attract widespread attention and this was stimulated by its uniform, a dashing military-style affair of a close-fitting scarlet
tunic with high collar and white Hussar loops and braid down the front,
worn with a navy blue bell-shaped riding skirt with three rows of white
braid round the hem, a hard-topped scarlet military cap with a black
patent leather peak trimmed with silver braid, black patent leather riding
boots, white gauntlet gloves and a white first-aid haversack and whistle.
This uniform, worn in 1909 by Miss L. A. M. Franklin, a prominent
member, is the only women's uniform among the hundreds of men's
displayed at the National Army Museum at Chelsea. At this time the
FANY's also wore the first and still the most elegant feminine mess uniform
on record. A fashionable white muslin dress was topped by a short
scarlet bolero, trimmed with pale blue at neckline and cuffs and with fine
frogging across the front. It was as pretty as a Regency fashion plate. One
of the boleros is still on show at today's headquarters.

In 1908 the FANY's drew up their constitution, thus becoming the first
women's voluntary corps to be established in Britain and beating the
Red Cross by a short lead. In 1909 they acquired their first ambulance, a
horse one, for which they borrowed Gamages' horses on Saturday
afternoons. The corps began to enter many sporting events. In 1909 they
won a cup at Ranelagh for good riding and expert horsemanship and also
took part in a military tournament and tattoo at Preston Park, along with
many army regiments. Ten officers and NCO's attended a smoking dinner
given by officers of the Blues in their mess and 'had a wonderful time'.

As numbers increased a more practical khaki uniform was introduced,
with shorter skirts, but the high-necked tunic remained. Next the girls

started riding astride, wearing a special skirt which by the unfastening of
rows of studs down front and back was adapted for this purpose, with
breeches worn underneath. Capt Baker disappeared from the scene, but
Col. Ricardo became Honorary Colonel of the corps, which rode weekly
with the Hussars. In 1913 they camped at Pirbright, with the Brigade of
Guards supplying all the necessary equipment and in general charge. In
1914, they went on manoeuvres with the army and officially attended the
Guards' church parade in uniform – the first women to be thus linked with
the army.

   In spite of all this the FANY's were rejected by the War Office when,
immediately war broke out in 1914, they offered their services. Fortu-
nately, like many other similar groups of women anxious to help in the
war effort, they were accepted by the Belgian Government and promptly
took charge of a hospital in Belgium. The British Government eventually
realised the need for and value of woman power and in 1916 the FANY's
were the first women to drive for the British Army.

79   Mrs St Clair Stobart took
her uniformed corps of women
to the Balkan War, 1912

By this time the FANY's had, of course, switched from horses to horse-power at the wheels of cars, and their driving 'started the employment of women other than nurses on active service', records Baroness Ward in her history of the Corps. By this time, too, they wore more practical uniforms for the job, with officer-type khaki military jackets, khaki shirts, collars and ties, and above-the-ankle walking skirts, completed by navy greatcoats piped with red. They became a fully-fledged unit of the Belgian army and also provided convoys for the French army during the war and in the post-war rehabilitation of Europe. Members won more than 100 decorations, including 16 Military Medals, one Legion of Honour and 30 Croix de Guerre. Alone of all the women's services they were not dis-banded after World War One, but continued in active existence.

Short-lived, but important in its time, was the Women's Sick and Wounded Convoy Corps, formed in 1907 by Mrs St Clair Stobart, with a training based on that of the RAMC. By 1910 they wore 'a very service-like blue-grey uniform and carried haversacks and water bottles. Their kit consisted of a divided skirt, Norfolk golf jacket and helmet'. They served in the 1912 Balkan war with the Bulgarians. In 1914 St Clair Stobart formed another body, the Women's National Service League, and when rejected by the Red Cross she went into action independently in Belgium and France, then went to Serbia with a team headed by seven doctors and ten trained nurses.

The refusal of the British government to make use of womanpower in 1914 did not reconcile women to doing nothing. At the outbreak of war the Hon. Eveline Haverfield formed the Women's Volunteer Reserve, putting her corps into khaki army-style uniform, the prototype of sub-sequent uniforms for women working with the army. Her women did much useful unpaid work. From the Reserve grew the Women's Legion, similarly uniformed. Members were hired by the War Department as cooks and waitresses. It was the first time in history that the army had paid for women's labour, apart from nursing.

1914, with its strange, heady atmosphere of jubilation and its anticipa-tion of early, easy victory, was a bonanza for women seeking a mission in life, an escape from the boredom of middle- and upper-class social involvements and a chance to show that they merited the full citizenship for which they had been clamouring. In their zeal for identification with the war effort they sought the outward and visible sign of their purpose by a strong insistence on uniforms. 'Uniforms, or hurriedly improvised semblances of uniforms, became a matter of honour and fashion, and if one could not manage a uniform, then an official-looking arm-band was *de rigeuer*', said David Mitchell, surveying the scene 50 years later in *Women on the Warpath*. 'In the music-halls, the stars of the day belted out rush patriotic numbers, the strapping chorus girls dressed as sailors and soldiers stamped and saluted with mock-military precision.'

The failure of the British authorities to make official use of women in the early days of the war led to a considerable number of determined women getting to the war in various capacities, usually under their own steam or by other forms of private enterprise. Thus when Dr Hecter Munro, a highly individualistic Scottish doctor and an ardent feminist, took his own ambulance unit to France in 1914, to work among the wounded, he included four women in his very unorthodox corps. 'Dr Hecter Munro', recalled novelist Sarah Broom Macnaughton, 'came in with his oddly dressed ladies. At first one was inclined to call them masqueraders in their knickerbockers and puttees and caps, but I believe they have done excellent work. It is a queer sight of war to see young, pretty girls in khaki and thick boots, fresh from the trenches where they have been picking up wounded men within a hundred yards of the enemy's lines and carrying them on stretchers. Wonderful little Valkyries in knickerbockers, I take off my hat to you.' Notable among these women at war was 18-year-old Mairi Chisholm, who worked with an older woman, Mrs Knocker, later Baroness de T'Serclaes, a trained nurse, right in the battle zone. They became known as 'the heroines of Pervyse' and, more simply, as 'the two'. American writer, Mary Roberts Rinehart, also described them. 'Under a khaki coloured leather coat they wore riding breeches and puttees and flannel shirts. They had knitted caps and great mittens to keep out the cold.' Both received the Military Medal in 1917, followed by the Cross of the Order of St John – which they received in their service uniforms.

The exploits of Sapper Dorothy Lawrence have more elements of school-girl bravado, TV farce and St Trinian's than of serious history of women at war. But they created a considerable stir and she notched up the distinction of being (so far as is known) the only woman to serve with the BEF in World War One. A hearty young woman, she had an invincible determination to get to the war and after failing to get herself appointed a war correspondent – for which she was one war too early – she reached Paris on her own. After a series of Biggles-like adventures and dressed in a private's smuggled uniform, she teamed up with working parties of engineers engaged in mine-laying as far up as front-line trenches, but after two weeks she was discovered through the perfidy of a sergeant to whom she confided her secret and was returned to London under special escort. The Defence of the Realm Act imposed a clamp-down on her story until after the war, when she wrote a book about it. She remained ebullient about her exploits, reckoning that in all six generals, 20 staff officers and numerous other officials had been involved in her army career. She quietened down, however, to the extent of continuing her war effort more peaceably in the less militant uniform of the Women's Land Army.

From mock-heroics to heroism marks the step to the career of Flora Sandes, one of the most notable of all women soldiers in the full masculine sense, and the first to become a commissioned officer in her own right in any modern army. She thus bridged the gap between past women soldiers in disguise and the accepted commissioned women in today's

80 Mrs Knocker and Mairi Chisholm in their sand-bagged front-line outpost at Pervyse, July 1917

81   Flora Sandes,
sergeant-major in the Serbian
army, January 1917, with the
Kara George medal

army. The daughter of a Suffolk vicar, she was in 1914 a bouncy spinster
of 38, working as a secretary but with some nursing experience. She went
to Serbia on 14 August 1914 with an ambulance unit, but after a tough
spell of nursing lost her unit in the hazards of retreat and became attached
to the Regimental Ambulance of a Serbian regiment. From this it was for
her only a small step to borrowing a rifle and starting to fight, as a few
Serbian peasant women were doing. She was at her own request enrolled
officially in the books of the 2nd or 'Iron' regiment and later was sworn in
and took the oath of allegiance, with other soldiers. 'Our Englishwoman'
was regarded as a kind of mascot by the soldiers whose life she shared,
though she enjoyed some privileges accorded to officers. Her appearance,
in breeches, man-style army tunic, knee-high military boots and close-
fitting cap, is familiar from photographs in the Imperial War Museum.

She was promoted to corporal, then to sergeant, went on fighting and
received the Kara George medal, the highest award in the Serbian army,
with promotion to sergeant major. After being wounded, she returned to
England for a time about Christmas 1917 and was received in full
uniform by Queen Alexandra, who showed great interest in her top boots
and revolver. She appeared at a gala performance at the Alhambra, ran a
fund-raising campaign and lectured to British troops in France.

She was back with her regiment for the final advance in August 1918
and was promoted lieutenant. She remained on active service in Serbia
until 1922, when she married a Russian officer, but continued to live in
Serbia as a civilian. She was called up in 1939 as a reservist, though she
was 63, but was interned by the Germans during World War Two. When
it was over the RAF flew her back to England, an elderly widow, and for the
next 10 years she lived in a Suffolk village near her childhood home.

Serbia was also the main sphere of activity of the Scottish Women's
Hospitals, another uniformed women's organisation which attracted
great attention for its heroic work, and also because of the magnetism of
its leader, Dr Elsie Inglis. A notable pioneer doctor, she was in 1914
practising in Edinburgh and also taking a prominent part in public affairs,
particularly the suffrage movement. When war broke out her offer of a
team of qualified medical women and trained nurses to help the sick and
wounded of the services was rejected by the War Office with the historic
sentence: 'My good lady, go home and sit still.' That triggered off the
determination that was to take the Scottish Women's Hospitals to many
fields of war. Over £200,000 was raised to equip these hospitals and
Belgium, France and Serbia all welcomed the offer of help. Later Corsica
and Russia also grasped at the opportunity.

In their uniform of Scottish 'hodden grey' skirt and the usual military-
style jacket, bronze-buttoned, with tartan flashes and the Scottish thistle
as their emblem, khaki shirt and tie and a grey felt Homburg hat banded
and cockaded in tartan, the women doctors and nurses of this group
stravaiged across Europe. They endured great privations unyieldingly, in
a determination to prove that women could surmount all the hazards and

difficulties that beset them, and with an absolute refusal to accept men helpers for even the heaviest work. Dr Inglis complained that the uniforms were shoddy and badly made by a London firm called Samuels.

Uniform as a symbol of solidarity of purpose and action seems to have been deeply rooted in Dr Inglis's mind from long before she donned that 'hodden grey'. When she was barely in her teens, between 1876–8, it was recorded of her later by her sister that at school in New Zealand, 'in the days when such things were practically unknown, Elsie Inglis instituted "school colours". They were very primitive, not beautiful hat bands but 2 inches of blue and white ribbon sewn on to a safety pin, and worn on the lapels of our coats. How proud we were of them.' Later, when attending the Charlotte Square School for Girls in Edinburgh, she showed her organising ability by pioneering a venture to obtain permission for the girls to play games in the famous square by canvassing all the residents for their permission. It was given, and her helpers in the endeavour were later called 'our first unit'.

She had also criticised the lack of uniforms at the Elizabeth Garrett Anderson Hospital when she worked there as a house surgeon in 1892, saying in a letter to her father that 'the nurses seem nice, but they don't have any special uniform, which I think is a pity; so they are pinks and greys and blues, and 20 different patterns of caps'. Her biographer and friend, Lady Frances Balfour, records that 'when a uniform became part of her equipment for work, she must have welcomed it with great enthusiasm. It is in the hodden grey with the tartan shoulder straps, and the thistles of Scotland that she will be clothed upon, in the memory of those who recall her presence.' It was 'dressed in her worn uniform coat, with the faded ribbons that had seen such good service', that she returned home to die in 1917.

The break-through to official recognition of women doctors in wartime was achieved by a group whose start was a historic moment in the story of women in uniform. When in September 1914 the first Women's Hospital Corps left Victoria station to take over the Hotel Claridge in Paris as a hospital, by arrangement with the French Red Cross, the group of women in green-grey uniforms and matching hats with small veils was headed by Dr Louisa Garrett Anderson, the chief surgeon, and Dr Flora Murray, administrator of the unit. Seeing them off was 80-year-old Dr Elizabeth Garrett Anderson, mother of Dr Louisa, who said: 'If you succeed you will put the Cause forward 100 years.' Without her the hospital might never have existed.

The unit did succeed in Paris, so well that it attracted the attention of the British War Office, which had resisted all offers of women doctors' help in army nursing. The unit was asked to organise a hospital at Wimereux, attached to the RAMC. 'It was', records Barbara McLaren, 'the first time that medical women had been singled out by the British Government and given equal responsibility with medical men.'

Success here led to the request, in February 1915, that Dr Garrett

82　Signed portrait of Dr Elsie Inglis in formal uniform

83   Edith Cavell in the uniform
she wore in her nursing career
in Belgium

Anderson and Dr Flora Murray should be entirely responsible for the projected Endell Street Hospital in London, a 17 ward military hospital which soon came under the charge of a complete all-women team of doctors, surgeons, pathologists, oculists, dentists, anaesthetists, nurses and orderlies.

To this early period of the war also belongs Edith Cavell, most famous of all nurses after Florence Nightingale and one whose life is even more full of paradoxes and misapprehensions. To start with, she was not a martyr, because, as her biographer, Dr A. E. Clerk-Kennedy, points out, martyrdom 'implies adherence to a path generally rejected', which is not applicable to her. Her 'crime' of helping more than 200 British and allied servicemen to escape through Belgium to neutral Holland made her more accurately the first heroine of the Resistance. That however, was not her main purpose in life, but almost an accident of fate. Her aim was to establish modern nursing in Belgium and she had done that before 1914.

The famous Trafalgar Square statue by Sir George Frampton is generally accepted as showing her as she was at the time of her execution by the Germans on 12 October 1915, but in it she is wearing the outdoor uniform of the London Hospital, to which she went for training as a nurse in 1896, at the age of 30, after working as a governess in Brussels. In 1898 she served as a private nurse at the Hospital for a year and this was the only time that she wore the uniform of the statue. After several nursing appointments in Britain she went to Brussels in 1907 as Directress of the Ecole d'Infirmières Diplomées there and in 1910 obtained the job after her own heart, becoming effectively matron of the newly-established Hospital of St Gilles, when state registration of nurses was introduced into Belgium. This gave her her coveted opportunity of reforming Belgian nursing. Part of her reform was the introduction of a uniform on London Hospital lines. The blue dresses with white aprons and white collars, detachable white lower sleeves and Sister Dora caps were a revolutionary change from the nuns' robes which had always been accepted nurses' wear. At first her nurses were pelted with clods of earth by Belgian workers and jeered at in words like: 'Ce n'est pas l'époque de carnival.' She herself took the matron's privilege of choosing her own uniform, a dark blue serge dress with a stiff white collar and a severe white cap with a deep turned-back peak. In the street she wore a long blue coat and a hat – never the London Hospital bonnet with strings.

At her trial she did not wear uniform, in order not to compromise her school or the nursing profession, and for this she was criticised in some quarters. Princess Marie de Croy, one of those accused with her, said: 'I regretted to see Miss Cavell in civilian clothes, a simple blue dress and a straw hat. It was the first time I had ever seen her out of nurse's uniform. It was a pity that she did not wear it during the trial as, apart from the significance in all eyes, anything in the way of uniform always impressed the German mind.' She refused to take any steps towards her defence, seemingly indifferent about it. 'She had been called there to start the

84 London Hospital-style uniform for the Brussels nurses trained by Edith Cavell, 1910–14

school and create a nursing profession in Belgium. She had done it. That was enough', comments Dr Clark-Kennedy.

She died in uniform. Her nurses, seeing her drive to her execution, 'caught a glimpse of Miss Cavell in her blue uniform sitting upright and looking straight in front of her'. When, after the war, her body was exhumed, it was 'easily recognisable by the uniform she had worn at her execution'.

8 | To war officially

85 A WAAC recruiting poster, end of 1916

As disillusion came and the war dragged on with its toil of death and devastation, manpower shortages became increasingly acute and women whose endeavours to help in the war effort had been spurned were sought out by the government and other authorities with a zeal exceeding their own. There was a phasing out of the 'loners' who, brave, foolhardy, dedicated or desperate, had been blazing so many trails through history up to this time, and the start of a vast regimentation of women which was to wind a continuous course on into the whole foreseeable future. But it was caused not by enlightened attitudes but the dire needs of the moment.

In December 1916 the first official entry of women into the services came with the formation of the Women's Army Auxiliary Corps when it was estimated that 12,000 men serving in back areas but urgently needed at the front could be replaced by women. The historic step was approved by the British Commander-in-Chief, Sir Douglas Haig. Mrs Chalmers Watson, a notable personality who was Edinburgh University's first woman MD (except for Dr James Barry), as well as the sister of Auckland and Eric Geddes, was appointed senior officer and Mrs (later Dame) Helen Gwynne-Vaughan, an outstanding scientist, became chief controller overseas. On 31 March 1917 the first draft of the WAAC landed in France, where it rapidly proved its worth. A khaki coat frock, more tailored and trim and more in line with fashion than would have been expected, was the uniform of the ranks and was a move away from the accepted idea that, as the army historian Major R. M. Barnes observed, where uniforms were concerned, 'those of the women who took over men's work are simply adaptations of the dress of soldiers'. Military-style khaki jackets were however, worn by officers and also by some drivers, with the long skirts of the time. The ranks wore pudding basin felt hats, the officers man-style peaked caps. By the end of the war 57,000 women had been members of the WAAC, which in May 1918 had been renamed Queen Mary's Army Auxiliary Corps, a tribute to its success. 10,000 of its members served in the Western theatre of war. They had, however, no military status and were still classified by the War Office as 'camp followers'. The corps came to an end in 1919.

In spite of the adventurous chronicles of earlier girls and women who ran away to sea in disguise and of sailors' wives who served valiantly, if unofficially, on naval vessels, the Royal Navy was slow to admit women. Not till 29 November 1917 did *The Times* carry an advertisement announcing the Navy's approval of women on various duties on shore which had hitherto been carried out by naval ratings and its decision 'to establish a Women's Royal Naval Service for this purpose. The members of this Service', it continued, 'will wear a distinctive uniform'. Up to then the doors had been firmly closed against women. Dame Vera Laughton Mathews, one of the first members of the WRNS and in World War Two its director from 1939–1946, recalled that in 1914 she had tried for a job at the Admiralty as a 'humble scribe', only to be told that 'we don't want any petticoats here'. She applied again on the very day the advertisement appeared, was seen by 'two ladies in plain clothes', and was accepted.

The plain clothes were significant, because until January 1918 there was no WRNS uniform and the girls, in civilian dress, were employed mainly as messengers, postwomen and waitresses in the officers' mess. When the uniforms came those for the ratings touched a new low for women's uniforms even then. They consisted of ankle-length dressing-gown style garments in thick, scratchy navy serge, buttoned up the front, with miniature sailor collars at uncomfortably high necks. The girls turned these back and borrowed real sailor collars from boyfriends for special occasions. The hat was the usual pudding basin, with a pleated crown. Heavy boots completed the outfit. Officers, on the other hand, fared better than usual, with a 1918 version of the very smart uniform they were to wear in the Second World War, which persists, with little except fashion changes, today. There were, of course, long skirts, but

WOMEN'S ROYAL NAVAL SERVICE
APPLY TO THE NEAREST EMPLOYMENT EXCHANGE

89　The original uniform of WRNS officers and ratings

there was something like tailored smartness and white shirts worn with collar and tie. Today's black velour felt tricorne hat for officers and petty officers dates from the start of the WRNS, but it was then much larger and heavier and had a matronly look. Hat badges and arm bands to designate the rank of the wearers were blue, not the naval men's gold.

During the First World War the WRNS force rose to about 7,000. The biggest innovation was the training of a group for wireless telegraphy, which proved highly successful and gave a lead to development in this respect in 1939. Other girls broke new ground – or rather water – and got near to the sea by acting as boats' crews. But in 1919 the WRNS too was disbanded, many members with only a week's pay. Nevertheless they formed an Association of Wrens in 1920 and, as already told, two years later became affiliated to the Girl Guides' Association, where they went into a more acceptable uniform.

The WAAC and the WRNS together formed the nucleus of the Women's Royal Air Force when, on 1 April 1918, by an amalgamation of the Royal Flying Corps and the Royal Naval Air Service, the RAF and with it the WAAF, the only women's force to have been created simultaneously with a men's one, came into being. A women's section was a logical appendage and to speed its creation members of the two existing services were given the opportunity to transfer to the new force. 10,000 did so, serving, like other recruits, as drivers, orderlies, typists, telephonists and store-keepers. Some were trained technically as fitters and riggers, acetylene welders and electricians. In all 32,000 women passed through the WRAF and over 300 served with the Air Force of Occupation in Cologne.

From its start until well into its revival in World War Two, the WRAF, later the WAAF and now again the WRAF, has been bedevilled by uniform problems. Its first members had already been provided with military khaki or naval blue uniforms, which it was decided had to be worn out,

with RAF badges attached to them and to the new working khaki overalls worn by the WRAF girls. New members were due to go into the RAF blue, but uniforms failed to materialise and there was much discontent among the girls, many of whom lived at home, 'had to come in by train and after working all day in their own clothes, saturated with oil and grease, they returned often wet through without any chance of being able to change', according to one historian. At a National Parade of Servicewomen on 29 June 1918, the WRAF was not represented, because they had no uniforms.

When, towards the end of the war, 700 members of the WAAC became waitresses for the Expeditionary Force Canteens, known as EFC they were the first women officially to help in providing the armed forces with food and victuals additional to basic service rations.

It would probably be invidious to describe either Kit Ross or *Pinafore*'s Buttercup as the first EFC girl, but it is a fact that the disappearance of women of her ilk left the British forces at the start of World War One without any official provision having been made for a co-ordinated canteen system, available everywhere on land and sea. In 1914, says NAAFI (Navy, Army and Air Force Institutes), the full-scale catering organisation for the services, which did not come into existence until 1921, 'a large British army entered the field without any official provision having been made for an accompanying canteen system'. Then EFC was created and was given Treasury and other loans. Women worked in it, and in due course the newly formed women's services became associated with it.

The Women's Land Army was formed in 1917 by the Ministry of Agriculture, when only three weeks' food was in stock for the whole country owing to the success of the U-boat blockade of Britain. The leading spirits in its formation were Mr Roland Prothero, later Lord

92 Land girl of World War One

93 Trousers strike a new note for women munition workers

Ernle, and Dame Merial Talbot. By 1918 land girls totalled 23,000 and their rather shaggy uniform of breeches, sweaters, smocks, gum boots and the inevitable round felt hats of the day was given clear identification by the armlets they wore. They did yeoman service in the literal sense of the word.

The women munition workers of World War One could claim, with justice, to rank among the women who, by wearing a uniform, showed that they were linked together in the war effort. The uniforms might be only the most usual khaki overalls and protective caps, but they meant something in a new entry of women into industry on a mass scale. It was in 1915 that the Government, hitherto deaf to women's appeals, went through the first big *volte face*. Ironically Mr Lloyd George, Minister of Munitions, called on Mrs Pankhurst of all people to recruit women for munitions – but at the outbreak of war the suffragettes had abandoned their campaign and flung themselves into the war effort, those in prison being reciprocally released. She responded with her usual *bravura* by organising a vast procession, for which the Government contributed £2,000. It took place on 17 July and it included contingents of uniformed women, including nurses, other war workers and 400 young women 'dressed in white and carrying crooks with red roses', plus a pageant of the Allies. The procession was two miles long, with 90 bands. It marched for two and a half hours through crowded London streets to be reviewed by Mr Lloyd George, on the Embankment, where 60,000 people had gathered to watch and to hear him. The effect on recruiting women for munitions was fantastic.

The call-up of men had made it essential that women should replace them in the factories. At the Government's Woolwich Arsenal at the beginning of the war there was not a single woman among the 14,000 workers. By 1916 there were 100,000 workers, half of them women, at the Arsenal and the satellite factories which had grown up round it. The employment of women in operating heavy machinery, as they now did, was something new. So was the fact that the new factory women came from all classes, including the professions, universities and even many whose names appeared in Debrett and who had never thought of working before. They worked side by side with traditional factory workers, and to a remarkable degree became 'mates'. At Woolwich they had at their head a notable personality, Dame Lilian Barker, woman superintendent. A powerful administrator, a martinet but also a real humanitarian, she was later to make her mark in the women's prison service. She had her own uniform, a severe round felt hat and a military-style jacket and long skirt, worn with collar and tie and all in khaki.

By 1917 an army of more than 700,000 women was employed in munition-making. Dr Christopher Addison, then Minister of Munitions, said in the House of Commons that between sixty and eighty per cent of all machine work of shells, fuses and trench warfare supplies were carried out by women. Mr F. G. Kellaway, MP Parliamentary Secretary to the

94 (*left*) Dame Lilian Barker

95 (*right*) Some of the women munition workers who helped to win the war

Ministry of Munitions, went further when he said that without the services of woman munition workers 'the Germans would by now have won the war'. Women's work covered practically the whole field of engineering and chemicals, from loading heavy trucks to highly intricate engineering and electrical operations. They constructed the chassis of heavy lorries and built aero engines, carried out hydraulic riveting, set their own tools, worked overhead cranes. Arnold Bennett commented on the elegance of their appearance, noting their uniform peg-topped trousers (for protection against high-explosive powder), but also the addition of fancy blouses and bright scarves.

Apart from the services and direct war work, women flocked into nearly every kind of men's jobs and wore their own versions of the uniforms which went with many of these jobs. They worked on the rail-ways as porters, ticket collectors, signalwomen; they served as postwomen, commissionaires, tram drivers and conductresses, and also as window cleaners, painters, chimney sweeps, lamp lighters, refuse collectors, usually in some kind of uniform. Most of them disappeared after the war, but today's women on the buses stem from the tramway women of the First World War. Glasgow was one of the pioneers of the employment of women here. Their Black Watch ankle-length skirts and navy service-type jackets were a model uniform for the time, worn with neat peaked

96 Women ticket collectors on the LSW railway: Norfolk jacket suits and large hats of current fashions of 1915

97 (centre) Page girl at a London hotel in 1915 wears a boy's jacket and cap, but ankle-length skirt

98 (right) London's first woman tram conductor, November 1915, Mrs G. Duncan

caps or hats, money bag and punch. Women porters were introduced into the Bank of England in 1919 but were abolished in 1921 because of 'the unsuitability of women to perform the work'.

Among the uniforms which came into great prominence in World War One and continued to be significant was that of the Red Cross nurse, wearing what has been described as 'the proudest badge', the Red Cross on a white ground. It had first appeared on nurses' uniforms in 1870, when the National Society for Aid to the Sick and Wounded sent help to casualties on both sides in the Franco-Prussian War. Contemporary pictures show nurses and other Red Cross volunteers at work. Like other nurses of the time the original Red Cross nurses had a uniform similar to that of the domestic servant of the day, but with Red Cross armbands, and one picture shows a head-dress similar to the later distinctive folded white linen square tied at the back of the neck. From then on the Red Cross nurse took part in most of the Colonial and European wars of the rest of the century. A Royal Charter of Incorporation was granted to the Red Cross in 1908. Local branches sprang up all over the country and gave training in first aid and elementary nursing. With the formation of the Territorial army in 1909 the Red Cross Society, with St John's Ambulance, was invited to train VAD detachments of men and women to supplement the TA's own medical services. This body of VAD's swung into action in 1914 and by the following year it had 200 detachments, with a total of 57,000 men and women.

The VAD women of World War One were among the first and most widely publicised women in uniform; their long blue cotton dresses and white aprons emblazoned with the Red Cross and their white head-squares became familiar everywhere. With the ever-mounting toll of war wounded they became increasingly necessary to relieve fully trained nurses from routine duties. Early in 1915 the War Office started to employ VAD's on contract in military hospitals for ancillary duties. Some 15,000 women worked in this way as clerks, dispensers and drivers as well as in nursing. The VAD's won fame, but not all of it was favourable. Many of them were animated by romantic ideas of ministering angels and took up the work 'expecting to hold the patient's hands and smooth their pillows while the regular nurses fetched and carried everything that looked or smelt disagreeable', commented Vera Brittain, who in *Testament of Youth* looked back on her life as a young VAD at this time. The regular nurses too 'were suspicious of the young, semi-trained amateurs upon whose assistance, they were beginning to realise with dismay, they would be obliged to depend for the duration of the war'. On the other hand, many VAD's lived in wretched conditions, as Vera Brittain did, working appallingly long hours for £20 a year, 'plus a tiny uniform allowance and the cost of our laundry'.

It took World War One to introduce women into the police force as uniformed members, though that is not quite all the early story. In 1946 Miss Dorothy Peto OBE, the first notable figure on the women's side of the police and woman superintendent for the Metropolitan Police force for most of the period of development between the wars, wrote an account, never published, of the women police. She noted that the first appointment of an English policewoman recorded in history was that of a woman Parish Constable in the reign of Elizabeth I. What her duties were is not known; probably she saw that the curfew was observed and she may have dealt with such matters as the imprisonment of women in the stocks. Had she a uniform? No one knows.

In more modern Britain women police got off to a slow start. The Metropolitan force pioneered them in 1907, but their strength for many years amounted to one notable but non-uniformed woman, Miss Eillid MacDougal. A former social worker, she was attached to the CID with the function of interviewing women and girls involved in sexual cases and managing a small hostel for such people. She continued to do this work, latterly with other CID women, drawn from the new uniformed force, until her retirement in 1932, and she played an important part in paving the way for women police. In Liverpool in 1910 a Mrs Hughes was appointed to carry out similar duties.

In 1913 Miss McDougall gave evidence before a Committee dealing with the Criminal Law Amendment Act, which in 1914 recommended that women police be appointed in all big cities to do work similar to hers. The war delayed the implementation of this, but it brought in the first uniformed 'policewomen'. They were not official, but a variety of volun-

99   Elegant, but short-lived. The uniform of 25 women porters at the Bank of England

100   Red Cross nurse, 1914–18

101   Members of a wartime
women's police patrol confer
with a regular policeman

tary patrols came into existence, operating mainly as protectors of women and girls in the West End of London, at railway termini, round army camps and at ordnance and munition factories and being to some degree linked with the male police force.

Two main bodies of patrols existed. The Voluntary Women Patrols, set up by the National Association of Women Workers, which later became the National Council of Women, had badges and carried cards of identification signed by the Commissioner for Police, Sir Edward Henry. Police officials helped with their training and some were employed part-time in the police forces under their superintendent, Mrs Theo Stanley, being paid for their work.

The Women Police Volunteers were organised at the start of the war by Miss Nina Boyle and Miss Margaret Damer Dawson, with the purpose of training women to become members of the police force. They fell apart, but were succeeded by Miss Damer Dawson's Women Police Service, with similar aims. She too secured Sir Edwards Henry's support and designed for her force a uniform of dark blue military-style tunic, collar and tie, worn with the long, full skirt of the time, with hard felt hats for rank and file and peaked caps for officers. The hat, she said 'was a lady's riding hat slightly modified. We thought it would stand the weather and might withstand a fairly sharp blow on the head.' Training included police procedures, first aid and even ju-jitsu.

Women patrols in general proved very effective during the war, but they never received official status. When, after the war, the idea of women in the police force was tentatively accepted, the new Commissioner of

102   Margaret Damer Dawson
(centre) and members of her
staff

103 Women police patrols on parade during the war, headed by Mrs Theo Stanley (*right*)

Police, Sir Nevil Macready, refused to recognise the existing groups and decided to recruit and train a nucleus of women police under his own supervision and that of the Home Office. Miss Damer Dawson's women continued to function unofficially, latterly under Miss Mary Allen, but were an embarrassment to officialdom and eventually disappeared. In 1921 summonses were successfully taken out against them for wearing uniforms too like those of the newly established Metropolitan women police.

Mrs Stanley was designated as head of the official venture, which started in November 1918 with an experimental force of 100 women, chosen by a selection board at Scotland Yard and intended as an addition to the Metropolitan Force. Sir Nevile's conception of their function was very limited. 'I don't think it is quite the thing', he said, 'for a full-blown constable to go and stir up ladies and gentlemen lying about in parks. It had far better be done by women police.' Rank-and-file policemen were on the whole hostile to the whole idea.

For the first appointments 25 young women, all of whom had been engaged in some kind of war work and many of whom had won decorations, were selected. Most of them had a strong sense of dedication, already shown in their wartime activities, and that attitude has persisted among policewomen. After six weeks' instruction, mainly at Peel House but with drill at Wellington Barracks under an ex-Guards sergeant, the recruits were sent to Harrods to have fittings for their uniforms. The

104   Lilian Wyles in the 1918
policewomen's uniform

choice of style had caused considerable concern. What happened and
how dire were the results has been described by one of the victims, Lilian
Wyles, BEM who, starting as one of the few women appointed a sergeant
straight away, rose to have a notable career in the CID, a branch she admitted to choosing in 1922 partly in order to escape from uniform. 'The
designing of a suitable uniform for policewomen had teased the minds of
the Home Secretary, Commissioner of Police and Mrs Stanley, our own
superintendent', she recalls. 'Time after time they sat in conference,
discussing the subject and examining sketches of styles submitted by
various firms, none of which were accepted. When at last the authorities
decided on a design of their own creating, Harrods was the firm chosen to
make these garments which were shortly to appear in all their ugliness on
the London streets. It was only the care taken in cutting and fitting that
made them at all presentable. Even so, they caused endless trouble and
profound dissatisfaction to Harrods' head fitter.'

The appearance of women in police uniform created a stir. 'For a
short time we were one of the sights of London, along with the Tower and
Westminster Abbey', continues Miss Wyles. They made their debut at a
police memorial service at the Abbey on 17 May 1919. 'The day previous
to the service our uniforms had been issued to us and included a pair of
heavy boots which laced to the knees, and were made of solid, unpolishable
leather, and a thick belt some two inches wide with which to span our
waists.' The boots, she later found out, were 'an old Land Army issue,
and had been considered too heavy for even that work'. Protests eventually resulted in their withdrawal in favour of boots which 'were made of
light leather, and were very nice and shapely'.

There were other horrors, repugnant to the new generation of women
who, in peace time, no longer felt that being in uniform was such a signal
honour that its style did not matter. 'All make-up had been strictly forbidden,' says Miss Wyles, 'and hair had to be severely dressed, in fact not
an atom, not even a stray end, showed itself from beneath the close-
fitting helmet, which looked so much like an inverted soup plate upon
the head.' The uniform, with its stand-up collar, had been thought
of entirely in terms of its masculine equivalent, as was usual at the time,
except that a skirt, long and cumbersome in the contemporary style,
replaced trousers. Queen Alexandra, with Princess Victoria, attended the
Westminster Abbey service and 'they were interested in us. To see six
women clothed almost exactly as men police officers, except for trousers,
must have been something of a surprise to those royal ladies. . . . As she
left Queen Alexandra gave us a sweet and encouraging smile which was as
balm to feelings frayed and strained by the inquisitive attentions of
London's public.'

The policewomen, however, even if they didn't accept the uniform,
soon came to be accepted. To start with, they patrolled in pairs in the
afternoons and evenings, with a couple of policemen following six yards
behind. That was necessary because until the Sex Discrimination

(Removal) Act of 1919 had been implemented women could not be attested and given the right of arrest. This did not happen till 1921, when there were 100 women in the 'Met'. In February 1922 they nearly disappeared, when the Geddes 'Axe' fell on public spending, but a nucleus was retained, thanks to a great effort headed by Mrs Stanley and reinforced in the House of Commons by Lady Astor and Mrs Wintringham and in the Lords by the Archbishop of Westminster. From this 'the women police of today were formed'.

Though the Metropolitan women's force grew and its establishment strength was 450 before 1939, actual numbers rose to only 245. The original uniform continued to be worn until after World War Two, with, however, a certain number of concessions, such as laced shoes and, above all, a jacket with lapels, worn with shirt, collar and tie. A meaningful development was the appointment of Miss Dorothy Peto in 1930 to the Commissioner's staff, with special responsibility for women, who up to then had been under the control of men. At first she was somewhat sidetracked by restrictions on her authority, but under Lord Trenchard she was given wider powers, with the rank of superintendent and appointment as an integrated member of the Metropolitan police administration headquarters. Under Lord Trenchard's liberal policy the status of women police was raised, and they began to enjoy something like similar training and conditions of service of service to those of men. It was not, however, until after World War Two that large-scale developments took place.

Outside the Metropolitan area the introduction of women into the police, their progress and conditions of work and also their uniforms were all dependent on the fact that police forces are largely autonomous, coming under the control of the chief constable of the area concerned, though with some guidance from the Home Office. Thus Birmingham and Sheffield had uniformed women policewomen in 1917 and by 1926 there were 100 policewomen in six county and 27 city and borough forces. Uniforms varied as did those of men, but there was, as today, an overriding similarity. Generally, the women had a mixed reception. A 1926 departmental report on their employment recorded equality with men in some areas, enthusiasm for them in Gloucestershire and Birmingham but advocacy of non-uniformed women in Liverpool. As early as 1930 a working party had recommended that a woman assistant inspector of constabulary should work with the team of men inspectors at the Home Office who regularly inspected police forces throughout the country. This was, however, not implemented until 1945.

9 | Developments between the wars

In the years between the wars the story of women's uniforms was somewhat disjointed, typical of an era of spasmodic efforts, of high hopes and anxious fears, progress and failure, false starts and brave endeavours, all overtaken by the holocaust of World War Two . . . yet today an era nostalgic in its bitter-sweetness, for sweetness is no more. With the winning of the war to end war it was natural that women who had gone into uniform for war work should shed it and the soaring unemployment of the late 'twenties and 'thirties also drove them out of the man's world of uniforms and into a woman's world, albeit an expanding one. A number of outstanding women were, however, convinced of the need for a small permanent force of servicewomen to be kept in existence in case of need. In the 1920s an Emergency Service was formed by Viscountess Trenchard, Dame Helen Gwynne-Vaughan and Miss Katherine Trefusis-Forbes and was recognised by the Army and Air Councils as providing a nucleus of women trained as officers for potential service. It supplied the leaders of the 1939 servicewomen.

After 1918 the FANY's alone took positive action to maintain their identity, and as a voluntary organisation were able to do so effectively. In 1919 they reorganised on a peace-time basis. From 1922 they trained drivers and practised signals work, with the co-operation of their old friends, the Guards, and the RAMC, and they retained their wartime uniforms. During the General Strike of 1926 the corps, alone of all women's organisations, was called upon to drive cars and lorries for the War Office and Scotland Yard, and also to drive ambulances. As a result it was, as announced in Army Orders of 14 April 1927, 'officially recognised by the Army Council as a voluntary reserve transport unit . . . at the disposal of the War Office for service in any national emergency'. It appeared in the Army list of that year, and has done so ever since, being the first women's unit to do so. In 1937 the name was changed to Women's Transport Services (FANY) because, as its honorary colonel, Sir Evan Carter, said: 'Both "Nursing" and "Yeomanry" are out of date and misleading.' The original name has, however, persisted, although from the mid 'twenties driving has been the corps' main function. Taking the

RASC Fulham tests, which meant that their driving was up to full army requirements, they also trained in signalling, wireless communications and military map-reading and thereby bridged the gap between the servicewomen of two wars.

Academic and various kinds of official dress took a spurt forward for women in the years between the wars. The decisive cause of this was the Sex Discrimination (Removal) Act which became law on 23 December 1919. Its first clause opened the doors of all uniformed civil professions to women when it declared that 'a person shall not be disqualified by sex or marriage from the exercise of any public function, or from being appointed to or holding any civil or judicial office or post or from carrying on any civil profession or vocation'.

Mrs Helena Normanton was called to the Bar in 1922, the first woman to achieve this, and in the same year was briefed in the High Court, to make a 'double' for women. In 1949 she and Miss Rose Heilbron became the first women KC's of the English Bar, though they had been anticipated by Miss Margaret Kidd at the Scottish Bar in 1948. The first woman judge was Mrs Elizabeth Lane, who became assistant recorder of Birmingham in 1953, by which time there were 500 British women barristers. Women were wearing legal robes and wigs for the first time – but the traditional ones, not feminine versions. In 1945 Miss Sybil Campbell became the first woman stipendiary magistrate, at Tower Bridge, but it was years before all the ramparts fell.

So far as the universities were concerned, the 1919 Act produced the capitulation of Oxford. Vera Brittain, a Somerville undergraduate at the time, recalls how in 1920 'on October 14th, I joined the crowds of young women in the Sheldonian Theatre to see the first Degree-giving in which women had taken part. Before the actual ceremony began, the five Principals of the women's societies – now all vanished from the Oxford limelight – became MA's by order of Convocation, and the theatre vibrated with youthful applause as they put on their robes and sat behind the Vice-Chancellor. . . . When the men, in turn, had received their degrees, renewed cheers echoed wildly to the vaulted roof as the first women stood before the Vice-Chancellor: among them were Dr Ivy Williams, Dorothy L. Sayers, and D. K. Broster, once at St Hilda's. . . . Even the unchanging passivity of Oxford beneath the hand of the centuries must surely, I thought, be a little stirred by the sight of the women's gowns and caps – those soft, black, pseudo-mortarboards with their deplorable habit of slipping over one eye – which were nevertheless the visible signs of a profound revolution.' It was the first time in Oxford history that these women, long-qualified, were allowed to wear cap and gown. In 1928, when Cambridge at last admitted women to full member-ship, among those who came to receive degrees long since won so far as examinations were concerned, but not awarded, was Dame Louisa Lumsden. She records in her memoirs, *Yellow Leaves*, how she went back to Cambridge in 1928, the last survivor of the five Girton pioneers,

105 The woman barrister was brought into the limelight by Margaret Lockwood's rôle as Harriet Peterson, QC in the TV series *Justice* in 1973–4

106 A new kind of uniform. Members of the Women's League of Health and Beauty in action, 1937

107 Today's uniform shows little change

to receive an MA Hons. degree in Classics won 55 years before.

Academically, women progressed conspicuously from this time and began to hold high positions in the universities. Notable was Dr Lilian Penson DBE, who in 1930 became professor of modern history at Bedford College, in 1938 Dean of the Faculty of Arts of London University, and in 1940 a member of the University Senate. Finally she was appointed Vice Chancellor in 1948, the first woman to hold this office in any university. But even today only one per cent of professors are women.

From policewomen to professors and on to physical fitness campaigners was all part of the variegated story of women in uniform in the 'thirties. When uniformed young people were starting to drill and parade martially all over Europe, the pacific Women's League of Health and Beauty grew from its original handful of devotees of Mrs Molly Bagot-Stack's system of exercises and body-training to attain by 1939 a membership of 160,000 throughout Britain and in the Commonwealth. The black satin shorts and white satin blouses which were its original uniform became the best-known of all women's uniforms of the time. They were ahead of their day in design and they are unique in that, though periodically updated, they are still basically unchanged, sharing a continuity which the League itself has maintained in its structure, purposes and even its personnel.

The League was a pioneer venture, anticipating a regard for physical fitness which was later to be seen as a social responsibility, developed under the NHS to an extent that has to some degree overshadowed the inspiration of the original one-woman enterprise. To Mrs Stack the system was also a philosophy. 'Surely the trained body can supply the secret of a simple happy life,' she wrote, 'for the body trained . . . is its own best doctor, masseur, pharmacopoeia.'

Unlike health and fitness movements in other countries, hers was not politically motivated, though she did once plant a flower-bed in the pattern 'Votes for Women'. She established the League in 1930, with sixteen members and a small money contribution from a committee she had formed to run her venture. The uniform was designed by her sister, Nan, a West End dress designer, and was the first to come from a fashion expert, though this was to become a feature of many future uniforms. The League emblem, a leaping figure, was based on a photograph of an early member, Peggy St Lo, who is still prominent in the League. The first public display took place in Hyde Park in June 1930 and membership soared into thousands, with further displays in Hyde Park and at the Albert Hall. In 1932 members paraded along Oxford Street in an outdoor uniform, also designed by Nan, consisting of a black velvet mini-skirt 30 years before its time, and a short matching cape, worn over the shorts and blouse. A military band and shepherding police were part of the procession. It created a sensation, and in a year or two membership was 30,000. There was a country-wide rally in 1934, with another parade and a Hyde Park display.

After Mrs Stack's untimely death in January 1935 the League was led by her 20-year-old daughter Prunella, who to this day remains the symbol of the League to all its members and is actively associated with its many activities. In 1935 the first overseas branches were formed in Canada and Australia. In 1936 the Queen attended the Albert Hall display and in 1937 5,000 members presented a display at Wembley Stadium, attended by the King and Queen. The League gained recognition by the Ministry of Education and the General Council of Physical Recreation. It also appeared, always in its black and white uniform, at international fitness rallies in various European countries. Prunella Stack became a member of the National Fitness Council, set up in 1937 by the Prime Minister, and of the Central Council of Physical Recreation. Mrs Stack's women in black and white were being officially recognised and membership rose to 100,000 in 1937. When, in October 1938, Prunella was married to Lord David Douglas-Hamilton at Glasgow Cathedral, it was a League event, for which Aunt Nan 'had designed a special uniform for the 16 picked members who represented the League at the wedding. She even saw to it that after the ceremony these girls followed immediately behind the bridal retinue, preceding the chief guests.'

World War Two inevitably disrupted the League, but in 1946 800 members took part in a Victory display at the Empire Pool, Wembley. The League became associated with the Outward Bound and Adventure Training schemes, where Prunella Stack was instrumental in activities being extended to include girls. Overseas links were strengthened and the League became a social as well as a health-and-fitness force.

Today, with 26,000 members in 160 centres, annual overseas rallies have become a main activity. A small annual Government grant helps training schemes. Classes are held for stores staff, schools, business houses, further educational institutions, retired women, and also at hospitals and for the handicapped. Members range from two and a half (in junior branches) to over 70 years of age. The black shorts and white blouses remain the usual uniform, but the shorts can be made of stretch nylon and the blouses of drip-dry nylon. Tights and slacks are, however, permitted for older members. In tune with the times is the recent innovation of a leotard, with white top and black leg sections in the uniform tradition.

Fashion in the 'twenties was geared to the young, with the 'flapper' as the new feminine ideal, the career girl to the fore and the 'boyish look' universally sought after. Corset and clothes manufacturers conspired to produce a bustless, waistless, hipless look, even among women who were not naturally made that way. As a spin-off from all this, the schoolgirl came into prominence and, for the first time, school uniforms began to have a fashion angle. The 20s and 30s were a period of great growth in girls' education and, says the *Centenary Review*, of the Girls' Public Day Schools Trust, the period 'brought greater cohesion to the corporate life of the schools exemplified by the proliferation of uniforms, blazers in

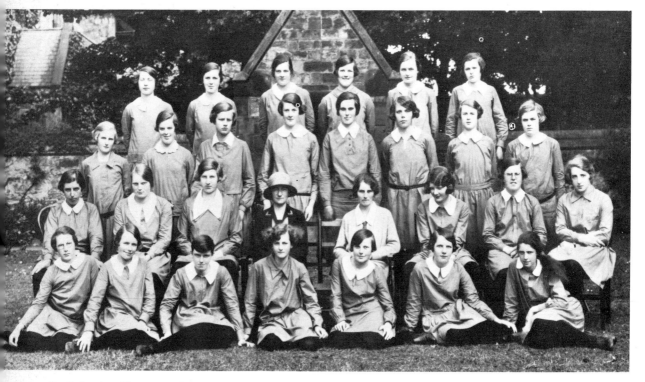

108 School uniforms caught the 'twenties look, with short skirts and hip-line belts

109 Women Black Shirts, Lady Mosley (*seated*) mother of Sir Oswald, with a member of the Fascist army

particular, a profusion of badges, and great enthusiasm for team games'. At this time, according to one report, 'tunics were as short as possible and girdles as low as possible, and for special occasions long black stockings were sewn to knitted tights to avoid a gap known as a "smile"'. Schoolgirl uniform had anticipated the adult stocking tights of the 1960s and with its hip-low girdle the gym tunic had become a fashion garment, which no uniform had done before.

One uniform worn by large numbers of women – and vastly more men – in the 1930s stands out from all others by virtue of having been banned, the only one, at least in the feminine area, to achieve this dubious distinction. The Black Shirts are almost forgotten today, but in the European political turmoils of the time Sir Oswald Mosley's British Union of Fascists, formed in 1932, loomed large. It not only attracted enormous numbers of people to its violent anti-Communist campaign and to what are claimed to be the largest political meetings ever held in Britain, but it also became the centre of constant riots and disturbances. On its formation, Sir Oswald recalls in his autobiography, 'it soon became clear that to win we had to wear some distinctive dress, a uniform in order to recognise each other. This is why people obliged to fight have worn uniform of some kind or other from the earliest days of human history. We wore coloured shirts for the same reason, and black was chosen not only because it was the opposite of red but because at that time it was worn by no one else in this country. A shirt is the easiest and cheapest garment for the purpose of recognition, and the shirts had to be paid for by the men themselves.' The shirt was classless: 'In the black shirt, the traditional duke's son and dustman could meet in the mess with complete equality.' At this time Mussolini's Black Shirts were on the march in Italy.

As militancy developed and attacks became a feature of meetings, with, Sir Oswald recalls, girl Fascists being knocked out at one Olympia meeting in 1934, a fully uniformed private army, of leading followers of the movement, was created, the first in Britain since Cromwell's day, with its barracks, the Black House, and even 'cups of tea prepared by women Black Shirts'. As a result, the Public Order Act of 1936 made the wearing of uniforms for political purposes illegal and therefore banned the wearing of the black shirts. 'The removal of the black shirt also removed the discipline of our movement', claimed Sir Oswald. The outbreak of war put an effective end to the movement; 800 Fascists were imprisoned, Sir Oswald for three and a half years. A black shirt for the last 20 years has been a fashion garment, and no more than that – but in 1974 IRA members were convicted for wearing black berets and dark glasses, claimed to have a similar political motivation.

By the 1930s general attitudes towards women in the services had changed and the lack of any women's territorial-type force caused anxiety among many women who had advanced greatly in all spheres of public life. No official move could be engineered, but a new Women's Legion was formed in 1934 under the leadership of Lady Londonderry, wife of the then Air Minister, with Dame Helen Gwynne-Vaughan as chairman. Plans for officer training were accepted by the War Office and Air Ministry in 1936 and both the Army and the Air Councils gave recognition to 'a voluntary organisation the purpose of which is to train women as officers for any women's corps that may be employed in duties other than nursing in a national emergency'.

With the Munich crisis the Women's Auxiliary Territorial Service came into being by Royal Warrant on 9 September 1938 under Dame Helen Gwynne-Vaughan. This meant that for the first time women were given official status as part of the army and ceased to be camp followers. From that time the ATS progressed apace, with companies formed all over the country. The khaki uniform consisted of a belted, pocketed army-type jacket, worn with a mid-calf khaki shirt, plus khaki shirt, collar and tie and a soft-crowned peaked cap. Officers had an updated version of the 1914–18 skirt and jacket. Both uniforms were reasonably becoming and well-made.

Camps were held to inculcate military procedure and atmosphere and by the eve of World War Two 17,000 ATS auxiliaries had enrolled, big-heartedly signing up voluntarily for the duration, without even knowing their rates of pay, which were not fixed until general mobilisation. Soon after the outbreak of war the Queen became Commandant-in-Chief and the Princess Royal became Controller for Yorkshire and, in August 1941, Controller Commandant. She frequently wore the uniform.

110   Dame Helen Gwynne-Vaughan watches a march-past of the ATS

111 The late Princess Royal visiting the ATS at an ordnance depot in the North of England

The ATS went to France at the end of winter 1939. Their telephonists manned the army telephone exchanges in Paris until the last minute before the city fell. They helped to re-equip the returning army after Dunkirk. Their categories rose from an original five to over 100. For the first time in army history women became carpenters, draughtsmen, electricians, mechanics, sheet metal workers, radiographers, welders and vulcanisers.

By a Defence Regulation dated 25 April 1941 the ATS was given equal military status with men – that is, they came under the Army Act and officers held the King's Commission instead of being only appointed to their ranks. Similar status was given to medical women serving with the RAMC, to the WAAF and also to women enrolled in the Army and Air Force Nursing Services.

Servicewomen became more and more involved in the war, notably manning ack-ack gun and searchlight batteries during the Blitz, and they went abroad, including the Middle East.

In December 1941 the National Service (No. 2) Act made unmarried women and childless widows liable for compulsory service with the armed forces for the first time in British history. Only those between 18 and 25 were conscripted, but this could have been extended to 30. A few conscientious objectors went to prison rather than don uniform. This Act also meant that women were eligible for all the traditional male service decorations, including the VC.

Conscription for women shook public opinion. In the perspective of history, even of recent history, it was a mighty revolution, but in fact

conscription of women into the armed forces was only an extension of the
direction of labour which had already conscripted them into war jobs in
industry. At a press conference in December 1943, the ATS Director, Chief
Controller L. V. L. E. Whateley, CBE, later DBE, stated that 'In the United
Kingdom there are more than 200,000 Auxiliaries and more than 6,000
officers. Nearly a third of the women serving in this country are trades-
women – that is to say, they have qualified in a skilled trade and are
directing, replacing and supplementing soldier craftsmen. In all there are
80 trades – 14 of them are "Group A" trades calling for highest qualifications – such trades as armourers, draughtswomen, fitters, and wireless
operators fall into this category.' On their uniforms they wore the zig-zag
flashes of electricians, the hammer and tongs of vehicle mechanics and
other insignia. There were, in addition, 15 types of clerk among the
30,000 clerks, 9,000 technical storewomen, 3,000 teleprinter operators
and 4,000 switchboard operators.

At the end of the war the ATS worked at SHAEF, wearing a special flash.
They were part of the highly organised super-combined operations team,
along with the Royal Navy and the WRNS, the RAF and the WAAF, the US
Army and its WACs. ATS operators put out all over the world General
Eisenhower's first D Day Communiqué on the Allied Landings in France.
They served with the British Liberation Army, were attached to the
advance section of Field Marshal Montgomery's Rear Headquarters of
the 2nd Army Group and were closer to the front and quicker in the wake
of the invading army than any previous women's corps had been.

112   US servicewomen of
World War Two

During all these activities their uniform acquired great variety, as did that of men. Battledress with slacks, dungarees, overalls, Wellington boots, leather jerkins, tin helmets all came into commission. Off parade a field-service cap could be worn, made in orange, brown and leaf green, but it had to be purchased by the wearer.

The ATS had its own bands and by the end of the war there were even ATS girls in a mixed Army bugle band composed of 12 auxiliaries and 5 RA buglers, with an ATS drum major, complete with leopard skin, followed by girl drummers and buglers in service dress, upstyled with white belts and gloves and special caps.

The inclusion of an ATS/FANY driving section in the revived women's army force dated from the Munich crisis of 1938, being agreed upon as the only way in which the FANY could be employed if war broke out. It meant an immediate 1,000 trained personnel for ATS driving, and with it went assurances by the War Office that the entity of the FANY would be preserved, its internal control and administration being maintained. 6,000 FANY's served in the ATS, wearing ATS uniform but with their own scarlet flashes. ATS FANY were responsible for training drivers at the training centre at Camberley. The National Service Act made them full ATS members, so the rest of their wartime story is the ATS one. It was at Camberley that in spring 1945 Princess Elizabeth, now Queen Elizabeth II, trained as an ATS driver and in motor mechanics, then joined a Senior NCO's class on maintenance, map reading and ATS administration, wearing rank and file uniform, becoming a junior officer and insisting on receiving no special privileges or favours. It gave a quite new turn to the story of Royal ladies in uniform.

As a voluntary organisation FANY also retained and financed their own headquarters in London, where 'free' FANY's pursued their own activities – a move that was to be highly important during the war. The 'free' women had their own khaki uniform, smarter than the army ones, with Sam Browne belts. More than 8,000 of them served in 22 countries during and after the war. Their most momentous work had, however, nothing to do with horses, nursing or cars and not till some years after the war did it become known. The sum of it was that the women heroines of the Resistance, who wrote a new chapter in the history of war as well as of women at war, were all enrolled as FANY's for cover-up purposes, were trained under FANY and wore the uniform of the corps during that training.

At the end of the war those who survived emerged as FANY's. Lise de Boussec came out of hiding in a French village to greet the American liberating army wearing her smart FANY uniform. Nancy Wake perhaps deserves the credit of being Britain's last woman soldier in the traditions of a man-only army, as she is the only woman on record to have led men into action during World War Two. Parachuted into France in February 1944, she became the accepted head of the 7,000 resistance fighters of the Auvergne, left leaderless by the hazards of the time. She was given the rank of captain, but could not wear her FANY uniform or badges of rank.

113   Princess Elizabeth, now Queen Elizabeth II, in ATS officer's uniform

Her general wear, says Russell Braddon, her biographer, was 'shapeless slacks and rough boots', but when, on 15 August 1944, 'the allies landed (rather belatedly) in the South of France and Germany's fate was sealed', she came out into the open. 'She carried the rank of Captain and her neat collar, khaki tie, her purposeful-looking army slacks and her obvious pride in at last being able to assume her true identity filled the Maquisards with delight. Wherever she was sent after that she was accorded all the privileges of her rank, salutes being not the least of them.'

Writing of the FANY part in the resistance Major-General Sir Colin Gubbins, CMG, DSO, MC, who had had a large share in organising it, said: 'To the organisation they were everything . . . without them we just couldn't have done it.' It was not till 4 April 1950 that the corps' association with the Resistance was revealed in a broadcast in a 'Now Let it be Told' series, by which time the film *Odette* was being made and was to give further recognition of the link.

In August 1938 the Board of Admiralty admitted the need for a corps of women to assist the Navy, but saw it at first as a civilian group. It was not till 21 February 1939 that Dame Vera Laughton Mathews was 'summoned to the Admiralty and appointed Director of the proposed revived WRNS'. In April advertisements for 1,500 WRNS appeared. It was laid down that 'the officers and ratings of the WRNS shall wear such uniforms as the Admiralty, in pursuance of His Majesty's pleasure, shall from time to time direct'. The officers had updated versions of the 1914 ones, but the unbuttoned top jacket button in the "Beatty tradition", became official, though it had earned Dame Vera a reproof from the Director in 1918. The ratings were given a new look, with neat navy suits and white shirt blouses, worn with collar and black tie. All ranks wore

114 (*left*) Recruiting poster for the WRNS in 1939

115 (*right*) Dame Vera Laughton Mathews (*centre*) inspecting Chief and Petty WRNS officers

opaque black stockings and reasonable laced shoes. A modified pudding basin hat was soon replaced by a sailor's cap, still worn. This was the style to which the Queen, now Queen Elizabeth the Queen Mother, gave her approval when a number of styles were submitted to her. She tried them all on at a Buckingham Palace mirror before making her decision. 'The children loved it', she said. This was the first women's service fashion to be adopted for civilian wear and it was a resounding success among all types of women. Caps of the naval style, in all colours and materials, were worn all through the war, and have come back into fashion repeatedly since then.

The first WRNS recruits were mainly drivers, packers, writers and domestic workers, with a few officers in charge and a few cypher officers in training. By the end of the war more than 100,000 women had served in the WRNS and there were ninety rating categories and 50 office categories, many of them involving highly skilled technical work on radar, communications, meteorology and radio. They served overseas in many theatres of war, including the Middle and Far East and WRNS cypher officers and coder ratings were the first women to serve afloat in the large troop-carrying ships.

They were not, however, given equivalent Navy rank to men nor did they wear the distinguishing marks of Naval officers, on the grounds that they could not discharge the full duties of Naval ranks and ratings. They were unique among the women's services in this respect and there were many disputes over the fact that they were denied the full status given to the ATS and the WAAF. The WRNS had their own code of regulations and they were not subject to the Naval Discipline Act – which Vice-Admiral Sir John Tyrwhitt, Bart. described as a 'compliment to their womanhood'.

The numerical peak was in September 1944, with 74,620 girls in blue. This dropped to 48,866 in December 1945 and by June 1946 there were only 15,000 left. But the service had proved its worth. On 8 May 1945, VE Day, an Admiralty General Message to all stations at home and abroad said: 'The Board of Admiralty wish to record their high appreciation of the part played by the Women's Royal Naval Service in support of the Fleet and in the work of the Naval Command throughout the war against Germany and her European allies. The loyalty, zeal and efficiency with which the officers and ratings of the Women's Royal Naval Service have shared the burdens and upheld the traditions of Naval Service through more than five and a half years of war have earned the gratitude of the Royal Navy.'

When, 25 years after the WRAF had been disbanded, the WAAF was reborn, history repeated itself in that it was formed from existing women's services. The 1938 ATS included 48 RAF companies, wearing khaki but with arm badges incorporating RAF wings. The Chief Commandant of the ATS argued that khaki would hinder recruitment to the Air Force, whereas 'blue uniform would not only encourage their loyalty and enthusiasm but would also be an aid to good discipline' – the main stimulus given by

116 Air Chief Commandant Katherine Trefusis-Forbes, wartime head of the WAAF

uniforms everywhere. In March 1939 it was agreed that airwomen should wear blue, but, however desirable this might be, 'there was not a stitch to be had'.

In spite of this the ATS companies were transferred to form the nucleus of the new WAAF. But 'for the first few months of war, airwomen were to be seen about in a strange medley of civilian clothing, aided here and there with an issue garment', says the official Air Ministry record of the WAAF. 'In fact,' it continued, 'it became necessary to recompense personnel for the wear and tear of their plain clothes. In December 1939, an allowance . . . was authorised of two shillings per week for the lack of a full outfit, ninepence per week for the lack of a raincoat.' Recruiting had even to be stopped for a time because of lack of uniforms. By April 1940 most members of the WAAF had one complete outfit, but it was months more before they were fully equipped. Katherine Bentley Beaumann describes in *Wings on her Shoulder* how the WAAF struggled along, trying 'to do credit to the RAF with no more than a black tie, blue overall, thick grey stockings, beret and badge'. At one point selected WAAF girls were sent out on a tour of West-end shops and wholesale warehouses in a desperate search for anything that could be adopted as uniform.

It took special agitation to acquire greatcoats for the girls in the winter of 1940 and to provide them with adequate supplies of shirts and collars and shoes. In April 1941 a working suit of battledress top and trousers was designed for the WAAF balloon operators. 'From that moment,' says the official record, 'practically every other trade presented a strong case for inclusion among those entitled to wear this suit.' The Duchess of Gloucester, gazetted an Air Commandant in 1940, frequently appeared in the formal uniform, and this had a considerable effect on recruiting and generally popularising the force.

While the struggle to equip the WAAF with uniforms was proceeding the force was expanding rapidly. From the original 2,000 members, consisting of one officer class and six trades, the force rose by 1943 to a peak total of 182,000 serving in 22 officer branches and 75 trades, at home and in nearly every overseas RAF station. As it grew, the WAAF continued to be completely integrated with the RAF, coming under its direct command and, as far as possible, under the same regulations. Uniforms were similar in style and materials except for the women's skirts and, unlike the other women's services of the time, the badges of rank of both women officers and airwomen were identical with those of the RAF men and the ranks corresponded closely.

At the height of the war the WAAF comprised 16 per cent of the strength of the RAF and 22 per cent of that of home commands. By the end of the war 95 per cent were replacing airmen, 70 per cent in skilled trades. They worked as drivers, orderlies, storekeepers, telephonists, riggers, fitters, acetylene welders and on radio location. They attended the same technical courses as men, and, like the men, they acquired the immense diversity of clothing by which the RAF broke through all accepted traditions of

117 The new WAAF uniform shown in a recruiting poster

118 Battledress top and trousers proved very popular with the WAAF

uniform, becoming a familiar sight in sheepskin jackets and trousers, sheepskin boots, anoraks, plus a diversity of protective and working clothes by means of which service uniforms were later to have a substantial effect upon civilian clothing.

The WAAF did not fly operationally, so their contribution to the story of women in aviation was to some degree secondary. Flying offers no known parallels to the women who went to sea with the navy or to war with the army in unofficial ways, though winged goddesses in legend had equality with winged gods and winged angels knew no sex discrimination. Marie Antoinette was the first Royal lady to fly, soaring aloft in a balloon at the end of the eighteenth century. France claims the first woman aeronaut in the person of Madame Blanchard. Later a Mrs Chisholm, says Stella Wolfe Murray, who studied the subject from its origins, claimed a similar honour for Britain, having more or less thumbed a lift from Lunardi when he came down near Glasgow. The first woman passenger in an aeroplane, according to aviation history expert Charles H. Gibbs-Smith, was Mrs O. Berg, an American, and the first qualified woman pilot was the French Baronne de Laroche, who received her 'brevet d'aeroplane' on 18 March 1910. In 1908 Wilber Wright had taken up women passengers and it is recorded that on one occasion he 'had considerable trouble with his three women passengers owing to the aerodynamic (and moral) hazards of their skirts, which had to be tied round with string below the knees'. Uniforms were obviously needed for women in the air.

Before World War One women were taking their pilot's licences. There was a set-back to women in commercial, and therefore uniformed, flying in the 1920s, when the International Commission for Air Navigation disallowed women from holding 'B' licences and also from any employment in the operating crews of commercial aircraft, even as air hostesses. This was rescinded in 1926 by the efforts of leading airwoman Mrs Elliott Lynn, later Lady Heath, aided by Lady Astor and Sir Samuel Hoare. Many women pilots became famous in the following years in commercial flying as well as in record-breaking flights, but they were loners, pioneering individualists.

The first women to fly for the Services were members of the Air Transport Auxiliary, the ATA, the wartime ferrying service which delivered planes of every type from the manufacturers to the RAF, thereby releasing thousands of young pilots for active service. The ATA grew out of the pre-war Civil Air Guard, which for a time had women members, represented by Mrs F. G. Miles, but it refused to accept women when it was re-formed as the ATA in September 1939 by Gerard d'Erlanger, with a nucleus of 23 pilots. Within that month official consideration was being given to the idea that 'we should obtain at least a dozen very capable women pilots'. Steps to do this proceeded through Pauline Gower, an exceptionally experienced woman pilot who had 'A' and 'B' licences, a navigator's licence and wide experience in running an 'air circus'.

On 1 January 1940 the first eight women pilots were accepted for the

ATA, with limited briefing to fly Tiger Moths. Ten more were added soon afterwards. Before long women were flying all types of non-operational aircraft and next they were going to the RAF Central Flying School for conversion courses on Masters and Oxfords. Uniform came into the picture as soon as they were accepted for the ATA, and an account of it was given by Lettice Curtis who, long afterwards, told the full story of the ATA and especially of women's part in it in her book *Forgotten Pilots*.

'Probably the most significant thing about the test,' she says, 'was that once we had passed, we could go and be fitted for a uniform. Up to this time we had been flying around in our own civilian clothing. Most of us did not even possess a pair of slacks . . . and therefore flew in skirts. To look as inconspicuous as possible I myself wore a navy blue permanently pleated skirt which I happened to own, a blue WAAF shirt – part of the official uniform – and a navy sweater. To keep myself warm in the air I wrapped myself in a teddy-bear cloth coat, tightly belted at the waist. We had, it is true, been issued with Sidcot suits, . . . but I never took to mine very much. . . . The first eight had been issued with the sheepskin Irving jackets and trousers as issued to RAF operational pilots . . . the jackets were a definite status symbol, . . . an affiliation with the heroes of the air!

'The Air Transport Auxiliary women's uniform consisted of a navy blue service type tunic with four large pockets, a belt with a large brass buckle and black composition buttons with a raised crown and the letters ATA. We were provided free with one skirt and one pair of slacks and when we went away we had to take the skirt, because, like the flying boots, we were only meant to wear our slacks on aerodromes. We were also provided with a great coat and a forage cap, thereafter the rest of the uniform consisting of black shoes and stockings, a black tie and RAF blue shirts we had to buy for ourselves. . . . The tunic carried one gold stripe on the shoulder for a second officer and two for a first and that, in the early days, was as far as the ranks went. For pilots there was also a pair of gold-embroidered wings.' Boots were unofficially worn everywhere, despite a rule about not wearing them off the airfield.

During 1940 women pilots rose to 26, among them being Amy Johnson, the famous record-breaking flier. She lost her life in the ATA, coming down in the Thames Estuary on 6 January 1941 when ferrying an Oxford. In July 1941 women, now more numerous, were cleared to fly operational aircraft, four of the original eight being trained for this, which meant that 'women were really on the way to taking a full part in the work of the ATA on an equal basis with the men'. By September 1941 twenty were flying Hurricanes and Spitfires, then they moved on to include Blenheims and Wellingtons and Mosquitoes in their delivery service. Conversion courses for four-engined bombers were the next development for the women pilots and by September 1942 eleven women were flying Stirlings and Halifaxes. Mixed ferry pools and equal pay were achieved in 1943, when women were flying Lancasters, the first Boeing, B17, and the Fortress.

There were 166 women pilots in the ATA, to 1,152 men, and four women

119 Women pilots of the ATA

flight engineers among the total 600 women personnel. Twelve women pilots, one woman flight engineer and one nursing sister were killed in the course of their duties. The total ATA deliveries of planes during the war was 308,567 of more than 200 types.

The ATA was run down in 1945, by which time women were flying Liberators, and on 30 November 1945 the ATA, 'unnoticed and unsung ceased to exist'. At the Victory Parade of 8 June 1945 in London 12 ATA men and 12 ATA women marched with transport workers instead of with the RAF they had served so well. It was regarded as an insult and when the ATA story was told it was entitled bitterly *Forgotten Pilots*, a record of achievement that neither then nor today has brought women a significant part in aviation as a whole.

The Women's Land Army was re-formed on 1 June 1939 and by September 1,000 members were at the ready, many of them already trained. They were part of the Ministry of Agriculture and Fisheries and the organisation was staffed and run by women, with Lady Denman, chairman of the Women's Institutes, as Hon. Director from the start and with seven regional officers. The uniform was businesslike and comprehensive – khaki breeches, shirts, green jerseys, brown felt slouch hats, boots and shoes of various kinds, overcoats with shoulder flashes, oilskins, mackintoshes. In all this plethora, the green armlet and metal badge marked WLA were the distinguishing marks of the army, and there was promotion to a special armlet after two years and to a scarlet one after four years. By 1944 696 hostels, with accommodation for 27,000 land girls and 230 staff were being run by this important contributor to the war effort.

120   The Women's Land Army revived

10 | Some uniforms that came to stay

The development of NAAFI was a between-wars story which paid off handsomely in World War Two. After World War One, in which arrangements for food and drink additional to basic regulation needs had still been inadequate and uncoordinated, a committee was set up by Sir Winston Churchill, Secretary of State for War, to advise on 'the kind of canteen organisation that would be needed for the peacetime armed forces'. It recommended a joint service organisation and a second committee urged that this should be permanent and capable of expansion in the event of war. The result was the setting up of the Navy, Army and Air Force Institutes, officially inaugurated on 1 January 1921 with all-over responsibility for the services and their accompanying families in the area of canteens, recreational facilities, shopping and, in fact, everything not served from official sources. It is a non-profit-making association, profits being ploughed back into welfare activities, and from the start it has also embraced a large area of public catering, from open days at military and naval stations to reorganising the staff catering of the Royal households in the 1930s. In 1939 55 per cent of its 5,500 staff were women, but uniform usually consisted only of overalls.

At the outbreak of war NAAFI went into instant action. Its civilian status presented problems overseas, where internal discipline and the Geneva Convention made it necessary for personnel to wear official uniforms. Therefore in the field men wore the RAOC uniform and women that of the ATS, both with flashes. The women were members of the ATS and held the same ranks. A main feature of NAAFI from then was the immense wartime expansion of the number of women in it. By October 1940 the strength was 21,000, with a strong preponderance of women. At its peak it had 110,000 members and by 1943 83 per cent were women, spread all over the world and doing all manner of jobs, from cooking and serving food and drink to running 10,000 shops and contributing largely to a business whose annual turnover rose from £8 million in 1939 to £182 million in 1945.

In the United Kingdom NAAFI staff were rated as civilians, and had their own uniforms. For women of junior staff rank it was a khaki skirt

122 Club assistant, 1974 style

and jacket with a cloth belt, epaulettes, bronze NAAFI buttons and badges. A cream cotton shirt and khaki tie were worn, and a khaki brimmed felt hat had the NAAFI badge. Khaki overcoat and stockings and brown shoes completed the outfit. Manageresses were similarly clad, but the material was better. Officials had suits of barathea with brass NAAFI buttons, cream tussore shirts and Henry Heath felt hats with the NAAFI colours, dark blue, red and light blue (for the three services) on the hat band and on their epaulettes. The chief woman officer had gold braid on her hat band.

There was one exception to this rule over uniforms. Because, it is said, General Eisenhower in the early stages of the war objected strongly to women in service uniforms, the many NAAFI women in North Africa wore the NAAFI uniform.

ENSA was an important branch of NAAFI during the war and stars of stage and screen, as well as thousands of other entertainers, also wore the same uniforms as NAAFI with their own flashes. So did entertainment officers and others involved in putting on shows of every kind for the troops. In one month in 1944 ENSA put on 13,200 stage shows and 20,000 films at a cost of £450,000 for servicemen and women everywhere and at war factories at home.

NAAFI naturally shrank after the war and today there are 15,000 men and women working in it all over the world, wherever British forces are stationed. NAAFI pioneered self-service shops in the early 1950s and they are to the fore in modern selling methods, with top business men co-operating with them. The women's uniforms have undergone a big change. 'The old type of uniform which had made the NAAFI girls look like

Little Orphan Annie,' says their historian, not quite justly, 'had undergone successive changes and was now redesigned to look smart as well as businesslike.' This means in practice that the girls in this country do not look military at all, but wear smart, well-cut overalls in the canteens and shops. Managerial staff wear civilian clothing, but where war conditions prevail, both go into updated service uniforms. In peacetime only men are attested or commissioned into the services, and therefore into khaki uniforms.

NAAFI girls have travelled the world in the last 20 years. During the Egypt crisis of 1952 they were included in the 600 volunteers who flew out to Egypt in NAAFI's biggest-ever air lift and they co-operated with that other redoubtable uniformed body of women, the WVS, in the care of service wives and children there. Korea, Cyprus and Jordan were other war or riot areas where they served in the 'fifties, the women, of course, as members of the WRAC/EFI, in army uniforms. In the 'sixties clubs, shops and welfare work grew and women restaurant and welfare superintendents became eligible for promotion to district managers. The successors of the vivandières and sutleresses have, via the uniformed NAAFI, become an important part of a vital area of service life everywhere.

Nurses achieved legal professional status only in 1919, with the passing of the Nurses' Registration Act. This provided for the first time protection for the nurse's uniform, badges and other insignia from being worn by unauthorised people. Further protection was given by the Chartered Association (Protection of Nurses and Uniforms) Bill of 1925. This was more important than it would be today, because, as the *Nursing Times* had said in 1909: 'So many people, with curious want of taste, persist in dressing their nursemaids in exact copies of hospital cloaks and bonnets.' As a result nurses were giving up the wearing of outdoor uniform.

State registration did not lead to the adoption of a national nurse's uniform. The intense traditional devotion to the uniform of the individual hospital persisted – and still does today. There was therefore still a great diversity of uniforms, but a general adherence to a coloured washable dress, white apron, cap, collar and cuffs. The Second World War, which, oddly, had a generally beneficial influence on fashion by ridding it of superfluous trimmings and giving it cleaner, simpler, 'austerity' lines, also led to changes for the better in nurses' uniforms. One example of how this happened was the London Hospital, whose matron at the time, Miss Clare Alexander, has recorded her experience of the problem; 'The new London Hospital uniform as designed in 1942 arose', she says, 'because it was impossible to provide the Nursing staff with frocks and capes under the old pattern, on the coupon allowance. I therefore went to Bradleys and they retained the basic pattern of the frocks, eliminated all gathers from the cuffs, bodices, skirts and aprons, did away with the old-fashioned starched upright collar, and produced the frock which is now worn by everyone. At the same time I started the uniform department at the hospital under Miss Wallace-Pennell, who

123 Nurse Thyra Larsen, elegant in 1910 uniform

124 A change for the 1930s

125 The new wartime uniforms of sister (*left*) and nurse (*right*) were smarter and more fashionable

126 The Army nurse's indoor and outdoor uniforms of World War Two. By E. Ibbotson

came from Bradleys and by buying better material, by introducing the coat instead of the double-decker cloak, we were able to save, in two years, 26,000 coupons which were returned to the Board of Trade.'

An equally interesting move followed this. Although hospital nurses liked their own uniform, a considerable number of SRN's, engaged in other kinds of work, had an SRN uniform. Miss Alexander provided a notable updated version of this after tackling her hospital uniforms. 'Following this little effort,' she continues, 'I became the Chairman of the Uniform Committee of the General Nursing Council and when the uniform for the State Registered Nurses was being revised, I got designs from Norman Hartnell for this uniform. Norman Hartnell had originally drawn the designs for Lady Louis Mountbatten, for the St John's nurse working overseas, but they were never used, and the General Nursing Council bought them. Then, with the help of Miss Wallace-Pennell and the uniform department of the London, we made up the frocks, aprons coats &c, for the State Registered Nurse of the General Nursing Council, and these were accepted by the Council.' There has been more updating since then, but the uniforms have continued to be fashion-orientated.

For service nurses World War Two played havoc with uniforms. To start with, there was a general relaxation of the starched look, with stiff collars, cuffs and belts giving way to soft, easily laundered ones. Nurses went into every theatre of war from the start, the first army sisters landing in France in September 1939. 1,300 nurses were evacuated with the BEF at Dunkirk and when Churchill and Montgomery took the salute at Tripoli in 1943 Queen Alexandra nurses marched past with the army. In 1941 nurses were given relative rank with other units of the women's forces, rising from Lieutenant (Sister) to Brigadier (Matron-in-Charge), as they do today.

But on active service nurses to a large degree went into khaki, like the troops and the ATS. 'Your Principal Matron visited a General Hospital this afternoon in Battle Dress and QA overcoat and storm cap', wrote the matron in question to Dame Katherine Jones, Matron-in-Chief of the QA nurses, from North Africa in 1942. 'I do wish', she continued, 'we could be allowed to wear khaki. The living conditions for most of the Sisters out here are very primitive; almost all are living in tents in ankle-deep mud . . . and smart grey and scarlet suits are most unsuitable. . . . I think the most suitable wear for the rainy season, two or three months, would be warm battle dress blouse and skirt to match and battle dress trousers for emergencies, the blouse to be taken off on nursing duty and a khaki smock put over skirt or trousers.' Later she wrote to her chief: 'I am very thankful that you have arranged to send us ATS uniform and clothing. I can't think of anything more suitable for this country.'

The RAF nursing service, which came into existence with the RAF in 1918, was recruited from the existing two services and VAD's. It received its royal charter in 1921 and in 1923 was given the title Princess Mary's RAF Nursing Service, which it still holds. Its members originally wore the familiar light blue nurse's dress with white apron and cap, or, for Sisters, the folded head square, but in the 1920s it took to the simpler white dress which had been adopted in 1921 for tropical wear. Sisters soon afterwards added a mini-cape in RAF blue. The matron's early dark blue dress remained almost unchanged until 1965. The outdoor uniform, in RAF blue, started with a suit with Norfolk-style jacket, worn in the years between the wars, but it then changed to a style closely corresponding to that of the

127 Pre-1939 uniform of Princess Mary's RAF nursing sisters

128 Red Cross nurses of World War Two, with updated uniforms

WRAF. This has continued, but a four-cornered hat, in black felt, has remained distinctive of the RAF nurses; it has been periodically updated.

Naval nurses, who first came into existence in 1884, were given the name Queen Alexandra's Royal Naval Nursing Service in 1922, when Her Majesty became their President. She approved the uniforms, which closely followed and still follow those of the WRNS so far as outdoor wear is concerned. But the working dress remains closer to that of the nursing profession, with a dress of sky blue, with apron and cap or folded head square. Sisters have a mini-cape in navy piped with red and their dress is also navy.

The Red Cross had a new wartime uniform, consisting of a navy blue gingham dress with short sleeves and a white turn-down collar, worn with an organdie cap which needed no starching or ironing. A square-bibbed apron with the Red Cross emblem was clipped to the dress with tabs, to get rid of the slippery shoulder straps. The reformed uniform was largely the work of Dame Joanna Cruickshank, first Matron-in-Chief of the Trained Nurses' department, a new unit of the Red Cross and St John organisation. She was largely responsible for organising trained nurses so that reserves were available for emergencies and volunteers trained for ancillary work. The VAD's loomed less large than in World War One, mainly because of this and the development of the services' own nursing services.

Although uniformed women members of the Fire Service of Britain made their first appearance in 1938 and might not exist today but for World War Two's call upon them, the involvement of women in fire-fighting, as in many other duties not normally associated with them in past centuries, goes back long before that. 'There is nothing new in women lending a hand in fire-fighting', said Commander Sir Aylmer Firebrace, CBE, RN (Retd), Chief of Fire Staff from 1941 7, in his *Fire Service Memories*, published in 1949. 'In bygone days', he continues, 'they used to man the bucket chains supplying their menfolk with water to throw on to the fire.' He added that the *Graphic* of 7 September 1889 shows a photograph of 'Some very hour-glassy women in uniform. The legend reads: "The Firewomen of the English Life Saving Brigade, taken at the Fire Service Congress at Paris".'

There was an all-woman fire brigade at Girton College, outside Cambridge, for at least fifty years, though it is doubtful if it achieved a complete uniform. The buildings were isolated and a local fire which blazed away unattended roused anxiety as to what would happen if fire broke out in the college. The first members of the all-girl brigade were trained by the famous Captain Shaw, who in 1861 had been appointed Chief Fire Officer of the Metropolitan Fire Brigade. He was far ahead of his time and achieved fame of another sort in *Iolanthe*:

> *O Captain Shaw*
> *Type of true love kept under!*
> *Could they brigade with cold cascade*
> *Quench my true love, I wonder!*

King Edward VII, as Prince of Wales, often visited his headquarters, wearing its uniform and attending a number of fires as a fireman.

When in 1937 the Home Office issued a statement that women might be introduced into the Fire Service not only as clerks but also for other duties, it came as a bombshell to the average fireman. 'For the fireman, the watchroom of a fire station had the same significance as did the bridge of a ship for a sailor. It was the nerve centre of the station and the idea of allowing women to cross the threshold disturbed one of the most deeply-rooted traditions of the service', said Mrs Betty Cuthbert CBE, now Lady Cuthbert, who was to become Britain's first Chief Woman Fire Officer and the wartime pioneer of women as permanent members of the Force.

Which station first employed women is not recorded, but the London County Council was the first large municipal authority to consider their employment in large numbers. It was also the first to form a uniformed women's branch, complete with its own officers and training instructors. Much of the credit for this belonged to Sir Aylmer, then Commander Firebrace, deputy chief officer, who in 1937 foresaw the need in the event of war. In February 1938 the London Fire Brigade was told to make arrangements for the large-scale recruitment of women on a voluntary unpaid basis, on the understanding that if war broke out they would be expected to serve full time. They would be members of an Auxiliary Fire Service, provided with a uniform and employed at all levels of control except at river stations.

In September 1939 this women's AFS went into action, its members being employed as drivers, watchroom workers and clerical assistants. Later cooks and dispatch riders were added. The women had their own officers, surprisingly given the same titles as men and were in complete charge of the women, except for finance.

The London AFS uniform was a matter of pride. 'Much thought and care had been taken over its design and, from 1938 onwards, the blue and red uniform, with its smart tunic buttoning at the neck . . . became a familiar sight in the streets of London', records Lady Cuthbert in a survey which proceeded to demonstrate the difficulties of obtaining uniforms in wartime. Plans to equip every auxiliary with a tunic, skirt or trousers, a cap and one pair of shoes had been made as early as spring 1938, with the addition of a top coat for drivers. But when recruiting soared on the outbreak of war supplies broke down, and hundreds of recruits were without uniforms for many months. Appeals to the Home Office were fruitless. The idea of collecting uniforms from women leaving the Fire Service and having them cleaned and reissued was highly unpopular. Existing uniforms were wearing out by 1940, when, says Lady Cuthbert, 'the old uniforms were mended and patched until they looked almost like patchwork quilts'. By the end of 1941, however, practically all firewomen were suitably uniformed. The idea that a new hat helped female morale resulted in a red and blue 'walking out' forage cap being introduced in May 1941 – but it had to be bought, for 6s. It sold well.

Uniforms elsewhere varied, some supplied by the Home Office and others by local authorities. But, generally speaking, they were ugly and badly made. Cotton overalls were sometimes all that was provided, but siren suits and duffle coats also appeared.

With the formation of the National Fire Service in May 1941 women ceased to be auxiliaries but, 'like the men, became full members of the Service', which 'did much to promote the pride of service and esprit de corps which became characteristic of the women in the service'. Numbers soared from 5,259 full-time women to 25,000 and then to 30,000 by September 1942. New categories were introduced, including wireless operators, dispatch riders, mechanics and hose repairers and promotion was extended. The Home Office had a Chief Woman Fire Officer, working to the Chief of Staff in all matters concerning women, the pioneer appointment being held by Mrs Cuthbert, who had joined the London AFS before the war as an auxiliary firewoman.

The standard uniform to be adopted by firewomen in the NFS was a matter of solemn discussion for several months. 'The main consideration', Lady Cuthbert records, 'was whether the neck of the uniform jacket should be of an open, closed or convertible type' and she adds that the uniform question engaged the personal attention of the Secretary of

State, who in November 1941 presided over part of a meeting at which those present included the Parliamentary Secretary to the Home Office, the Principal Assistant Under Secretary of the Fire Service Department, the Chief of Fire Staff and the Chief Woman Fire Officer. Four firewomen paraded in various types of uniform worn by members of the AFS brigades and the Civil Defence Services. The Minister's preference for an open-neck or convertible neck tunic led to the adoption of the latter, as in Civil Defence uniforms. The material for jacket, skirt and overcoat was navy gabardine, the style that of London but later changed to the Civil Defence pattern because of continued supply difficulties. Trousers were skiing type, to fit inside rubber boots, and were therefore different from the slacks of the other women's services. Later Civil Defence styles had to be adopted. The cap was also of skiing style, with the forage cap retained as an optional paid-for alternative.

When women were first drafted into the Fire Service in 1942 as a measure of conscription, the supply of uniforms became even worse, and later in 1943 many women had nothing at all except overalls, helmet and respirator. 'The work of instilling a sense of discipline and esprit de corps into large numbers of recruits was made doubly difficult by the lack of uniform among all ranks', comments Lady Cuthbert. It went on for a long time. By 30 June 1942 out of a total of 26,606 firewomen, only 11,284 had been issued with uniform. The cap shrunk and had to be replaced by a new design. Battle dress tops were introduced in 1943 for the comfort of drivers. All sorts of special equipment was also needed – dungarees, goggles, rubber boots. From junior officers came complaints that their

129   Review of NFS women by Queen Elizabeth the Queen Mother, accompanied by Princess Elizabeth, now Queen Elizabeth II, during the war

130   Miss V. M. Garner, MBE

131   New 1966 uniform for
ranks below officer level

uniforms were a half-way house between the ranks and their superiors, so ATS officer-style jackets were introduced. Caps were hard, so a new lighter, more feminine style replaced the masculine peaked one. Shoulder badges, introduced in 1943, had to be private purchases.

There were, however, touches of elegance. Women officers of and above the rank of assistant area officer had an embroidered cap badge with oak leaves surrounding the NFS star. Breast badges and shoulder badges of rank were also worn. The chief woman fire officer had a distinguishing row of silver oak leaves round her cap peak and three silver sleeve stripes, with red bands between them, and a small impeller above the stripes. Other officers had smaller versions of this.

The NFS women faded away rapidly at the end of the war. There were 27,300 in September 1943, but only 4,400 by 1945. But some of the war-time women stayed on – and a small number of them are still there 30 years on. The establishment of 500 women in 1948 has risen to over 1,000, with some 50 women staff officers. In 1948 Miss Violet Garner MBE, who had entered the AFS as a wartime recruit, was appointed at the Home Office to watch the interests of women in the Fire Service, being upgraded to Assistant Inspector of the Fire Services in 1965, with equal status with nine male colleagues.

Uniforms for women have been periodically restyled. In 1966 there was a major review of the uniforms of both men and women officers and firewomen, bringing them generally in line with those of policewomen. A shaped jacket in good quality gabardine and a fashion-length skirt are worn by officers, with collar and tie and a peaked cap. For the ranks, a double-breasted jacket and neat skirt, also worn with collar and tie, and a new-style forage cap to replace the peaked style, have been introduced. Fashion designer Jean Allen acted as consultant. Now a further review is under way the aim being to modernize the uniform in both style and material and to introduce a new-style cap.

At the end of 1973 the authorised establishment for women in fire brigades in England and Wales was 1,075.

All women members of fire brigades are uniformed, but those in administrative jobs are not, nor are their men colleagues. 'Psychologically uniform helps discipline, and the Fire Service is necessarily under firm discipline', says Miss Garner. 'Delays or errors may mean loss of life. Women fire officers and rank and file also come in contact with the public in various capacities, and their uniform brings confidence and reassurance to wearer and public alike.'

Civil defence workers shed their uniforms and their association with their wartime work as soon as peace came. Chief of them were the ARP personnel, who included women of all ages, from teenagers to those in their sixties. It was a vast and intricate countrywide network, with small First Aid posts set up everywhere and anywhere and with air raid shelters in all kinds of places, from London Underground stations to rough shacks. The women's uniform was navy, including a trouser and jacket

suit and a navy heavy cotton overall, with, of course, a tin helmet and a
special gas mask – an item never used, any more than were the millions of
civilian ones systematically distributed at the onset of war. The numbers
involved in this branch of civil defence are hard to estimate, but in 1942
there were more than 80,000 full-time women wardens, ambulance
drivers, storekeepers and firewomen in First Aid posts and rest centres,
plus 350,000 part-time CD women workers.

Uniforms, as in the first World War, also spread into many of the civil
occupations where women replaced men and in many of which they remained after the war. As in World War One, transport absorbed many of
them. Buses had largely replaced trams, and Birmingham had 600
women bus conductors, in smart dark blue uniforms consisting of tunics
and divided skirts – an idea so practical that one wonders why it was not
more generally adopted at a time when trousers for women were not so
widely accepted as in recent years. These women also had caps and
gaiters, overcoats and mackintoshes. Other cities and towns which were
prominent in having women on their buses were Glasgow, Harrogate,
Manchester, Leicester, Birmingham, Wolverhampton, Walsall and
Burton-upon-Trent. There was a great rush of girls and women wanting
to go on the London buses, but owing to the evacuation of so many people
from the capital the services were curtailed; it was not until 1940 that
openings became available and then only by gradual stages. From then,
however, the woman bus conductor has become an accepted category of
women in uniform – though one given to her own variations on the strict
outfit; the only one, probably, to combine her uniform with her own
head-scarf, sandals and all kinds of blouses and jumpers.

Munition workers reached their peak in 1943, when nearly two million
women were employed in iron and steel, shipbuilding, engineering, and
the making of tanks, aircraft, chemicals and explosives. Five million were
engaged during the war in 'other work' apart from direct war activities.
Uniforms varied from overalls to service-style outfits.

Of all the women's uniforms which originated in World War Two that
of the Women's Voluntary Service, which in 1966 received the Royal
Warrant and became the Women's Royal Voluntary Service, is uniquely
significant in that it symbolises a union of the oldest and the newest
concepts of women's services for the community. Its members can be
seen as the successors and modern equivalents of the time-honoured
ministering angel, the Lady Bountiful, the benevolent helping hand
stretched out to help the sick, the old and the needy. But they were
basically different. Their founder, Stella Lady Reading, was emphatic
about this and, as an article on her work pointed out in 1972, she 'stressed
that voluntary service had been the prerogative of the wealthy until the
WVS brought it within the reach of all; that has given a sense of responsibility to women who had never thought of influencing the life of the
community beyond their doorsteps. She had uncanny ability to anticipate
social trends and new needs that could be met by her members.'

132 A girl air raid warden;
Sylvia Marriott

The WVS was established in 1938, when Lady Reading, a woman with a notable record in public life and a business background, was urged by Sir Samuel Hoare, then Home Secretary, to set up a women's organisation for the purpose of recruiting women into ARP (Air Raid Precautions), where at that time they held a very minor place. She accepted the assignment, visualising a country-wide network embracing the Home Office, local authorities and the main existing women's organisations. The WVS came into existence in Spring 1938 and on 18 June it got off the ground at a press conference held at the House of Commons.

From the start it laid down certain rules, chief of which was that there were to be no ranks or commissions, no socially orientated activities, but a concentration of all available energies, abilities and time to the service of the community on a basis of trained efficiency. That principle remains.

How opportune and right was Lady Reading's version was shown by the fact that within a year the WVS had 300,000 members. They have always been unpaid. There is no subscription, but membership involves undertaking certain services and basic training. The adoption of a uniform was implicit in her concept. A uniform did away with social barriers and signified the job, not the individual who did it. It was a leveller among the very varied women involved. There was, however, a problem; the compulsory wearing of uniform would be contrary to the spirit of a voluntary service, so there has never been such compulsion.

In an article, *Service in the New Decade*, written shortly before her death in 1971, Lady Reading summed up the uniform question as she saw it after more than 30 years of WVS – and WRVS – history. 'There are many people', she wrote, 'who think that the wearing of uniform is an anachronism and who in fact are rather put off by the idea of a service where uniform is worn. . . . Over the years the WRVS has become firmly established in the public mind as the "Women in Green", the women who come along and help in times of difficulty. . . . The uniform is workmanlike and has been designed in order to enable the wearer to do the job. Somehow the WRVS has succeeded in wearing a uniform without looking regimented.'

The grey-green uniform, quickly adopted by the WVS in 1938, was the result of an invitation to a number of leading London dressmakers to present designs for a tweed coat and skirt, a greatcoat, a dress, a jumper and a hat. A committee of four was appointed to make the final choice, the designers' names being withheld. Couturier Digby Morton's classic suit and coat were the chosen basics and his expertise as a suit designer was shown by his breakaway from the military conception which still dominated women's uniforms at the time. The colour selected was reached by a process of elimination. Blue, khaki, black and brown had already been chosen by the women of the WAAF, WRNS, ATS, St John's Ambulance and the Land Army. The best remaining choice seemed to be green. Owing to superstition grey was woven into it, which had the additional advantage of making the colour more serviceable. A Scottish firm, chosen by Lady

133   Wartime WVS woman, as seen in a statuette by Keith Godwin, ARCA

Reading, made all the suits and coats until 1971, originally in a size range from 8 to 26, but later from 12 to 24. Now a London firm has taken over production.

The plain jumper and short-sleeved blouse, both in classic style, were in cherry red, which was also used for the band on the 'schoolgirl' green felt hat. When Sir Winston Churchill first saw a march past of the WVS he said in disgust: 'Look at your girls. Each hat is worn at a different angle.' Lady Reading's firm reply was: 'Here is a sense of individuality in operation, but uniformity of pattern', which was the core of her policy for the WVS. Perhaps it should be the ideal of all uniforms. The varied hat angles were thus 'part of the original concept – that the WVS should do the same job in different ways, each of them translating their personality into it'. King George VI once said to a member: 'Aren't you going to have uniform?' to which the embarrassed reply was: 'Yes, sir, actually I am wearing one.' The unobtrusive suit was useful off-duty for women who combined their service with home responsibilities. Later on, gabardine and linen uniforms were designed for overseas service – and the members all paid for their own uniforms.

At its wartime peak the WVS had a million members of which only 200 were paid staff. The ratio has been maintained, and it has become interwoven with the community services. As activities have changed in a changing world, the uniform has also moved with the times. The heavy tweed suit has given place to an updated one in fine worsted. A practical car coat has been added. A short and a long-sleeved dress, shirt-waister style, are made in Dacron jersey in a soft green, plus a cotton version for summer. The shirt blouse and jersey, now matched with a cardigan, are smarter. The hat is a shapely Trilby style in soft green felt, which Sir Winston Churchill would admire. A new-style green beret, with a red pom-pom on top, is another change, a concession to the more relaxed and feminine look of today's uniforms. New too, is a smart trouser suit in bonded green polyester, added in 1972 and approved as uniform for all but the most formal occasions. A shoulder bag, large hand-bag and a brief case are other additions. There is a uniform department at headquarters in Park Lane, but 75 per cent of the business of this 'shop' is done by mail order, from catalogues and price-lists supplied to all branches.

Members still buy their own uniforms. The organisation is still non-profit-making, but is aided by donations and bequests. It is controlled by a policy-framing committee headed by the Chairman, and an advisory council on which 82 women's organisations are represented. It is today the biggest of all women's voluntary organisations, with a roll-call of about 500,000. It has twelve regional directors and a structure which enables it to swing into instant large-scale action in any emergency. It lives up to the description 'the most remarkable women's organisation in history'.

134 The Meals on Wheels Service, Hertfordshire, 1963

11 | A new look for traditional uniforms

135　Two policewomen registering at a London Labour Exchange in 1941 for war work

Nationally it took World War Two to give a real spurt to the development of women police. The regular women were supplemented by the Women's Auxiliary Police Corps, with 342 attested members, and it did valuable work. But although a working party had recommended as long ago as 1930 that a woman assistant inspector of constabulary should be appointed to work with the team of men inspectors at the Home Office who regularly inspected police forces all over the country, it was not until 1945 that this was done. Miss Barbara Denis de Vitré, OBE, who had been a member of the police since 1928, was the first woman staff officer to the Inspectorate of Constabulary from 1945 to 1948 and the first woman assistant inspector of constabulary from then until her death in 1960. The post was maintained and today Miss Jean S. Law, OBE, assistant inspector, and two staff officers represent women police at the Home Office.

It is symptomatic of slow development at the top that women police waited many years for the real updating of their uniform; the first big change did not come till 1946. Mrs Shirley Becke, OBE, QPM from 1966 to 1974 a commander in the Metropolitan Police and the first woman to attain this rank, joined the force in 1941 and recalls her early uniform. It was of navy serge, basically still very like the 1919 style. The prescribed skirt length was 14 inches from the ground, regardless of height. As this was too long for Mrs Becke's 6 ft 1 in. she shortened it herself, and many others did the same. In addition to this formal uniform, there was a second one in heavy serge, known by the wearers as 'fluffies'. Two overcoats were provided, heavy and light. The heavy one was double-breasted and there was a strict instruction that it should be buttoned to left and right alternately at two months' intervals, to ensure even wear. Laced-up boots were still worn but with 'fluffies' shoes were permitted. Boots were made by Manfields in Piccadilly with individual lasts for each policewoman, so that 'they fitted like gloves', recalls Mrs Becke.

This was the final Peto uniform, but a change came in 1946 when Miss E. C. Bather OBE took over from Miss Peto as superintendent for the Metropolitan Police until 1961. Fresh from six years in the WAAF, she introduced a suit with service-style jacket which was worn from 1946 till 1967, with skirt and jacket lengths varying according to fashion. A peaked military cap replaced the variety of topees that had lasted for nearly 30 years, except when ousted by the wartime tin helmets, which the wearers preferred as being kinder to hair styles. Miss Bather also won for women in the 'Met' the privilege of having their uniforms individually tailored, in return for waiving the yearly issue in favour of renewals when needed. The opaque woollen or lisle stockings of the Peto uniform were replaced by see-through nylons – for the first time part of the clothing issue. Lord Morrison, Home Secretary, had even said 'that a reasonable degree of non-aggressive lipstick and "make up" should be permitted' – but did not specify at what point aggression came in!

In 1967, with Commander Becke as head of the women police, Sir John Waldron, later Commissioner of the Metropolitan Force, called in Norman Hartnell to design a new-look uniform for the 'Met' women, specifying that it should 'fit and flatter women aged from 19 to 55, from 5 ft 4 in. to 6 ft 1 in., from the very thin to the very fat'. Mrs Becke pointed out to Mr Hartnell that there must also be pockets galore, because handbags had not yet arrived. Thus emerged the Becke uniform, only the third in nearly 40 years. The Hartnell barathea suit, with boxy jacket, close double row of buttons, velvet collar, high revers and slit pockets was a big breakaway from fixed ideas on uniforms. The white shirt had a cutaway collar worn with a bow instead of the masculine tie. The heavy greatcoat was replaced by a cape – a becoming adaptation of the original policeman's cape. Shoes could be black court style, except on patrol and a few other duties, when laced walking ones continued. The new hat was designed by Royal milliner Simone Mirman and it too was aimed at being universally becoming, with a sophisticated pill-box crown, a small patent leather peak and, of course, the police badge. Senior officers had larger badges, plus a line of braid round the peak – black for chief inspectors and silver for superintendents and higher ranks.

With this new image for the policewoman the system by which their uniforms were chosen and updated was changed countrywide. A working party set up by the Home Office to consider women's uniforms and give a lead included representatives of local authorities. To start with, it recommended the Hartnell uniform, but unfortunately the bespoke style did not adapt to the ready-to-wear manufacture needed for countrywide use. Finally the Surrey uniform was chosen by selection from many existing ones and was recommended for all forces in 1973. It was amenable to large-scale production and its slightly waisted, single-breasted jacket and A-line skirt were fashionable and flattering. The Surrey hat was also chosen, with its stitched peak, slightly high white crown and diced hat band. This last feature was recommended to all police forces as a means of identifying them, whether men or women, from the many other groups who were by now wearing navy blue uniforms of contemporary style. Skirts were to be at least to the knee – but, as ever, they tend to creep up. Women police in the Traffic Division and dog handlers wear trouser suits

136 WPC 550 Jennings, later Commander Shirley Becke, in Piccadilly Circus, 1942–3, in wartime uniform

137 The 1946 uniform, on military lines

138 The Norman Hartnell uniform, 1966, brought elegance to Metropolitan policewomen

139 (*right*) The Metropolitan policewoman of 1974

140 Woman prison officer, 1947

with hip-length single-breasted jackets. The shoulder bag is now general, and it holds the personal radio, with the aerial coming out through the strap. The Hartnell cape remains in the Metropolitan force, plus a light-weight showerproof coat. An allowance for nylons is given to all ranks. In 1971 there was an ironic flash-back to early dress troubles when boots were begged for and approved – knee-high, low-heeled, in black leather – but fashion boots now. Jewellery is still barred, except for engagement and wedding rings, but restrained make-up is approved. Hair has to clear the collar, but for the long-haired a French pleat is approved. A feature of the working party's recommendations is that uniforms are to be kept under review in the light of fashion as well as function.

There are nearly 5,000 policewomen now in Great Britain, and though this is less than 5 per cent of the total force of 99,942 the women are accepted and approved. In February 1973 the 'Met' abolished its separate establishment for women and integrated them completely within the force. This meant, says Commander Becke, that promotion for women was now in competition with the 25,050 policemen in the force. On her retirement in May 1974, a successor, Daphne Skillern, was appointed with the same rank.

Although prison matrons were introduced by Elizabeth Fry as a basic part of her scheme for prison reform, and were given official status by Sir Robert Peel in an act of 1823, only comparatively recently have women achieved real standing and authority, designated by full uniform, in the prison service. Peel's decree that women prisoners should not be looked after entirely by men officers was, however, implemented. A photograph of such women at Preston prison (no longer in existence) in 1842 show a group of women prison staff in what approximated to uniform at that time – dark dresses with white collars and bonnets which may indicate different grades.

Matrons still look after women prisoners in police courts, in addition to women police, but the first record of women being appointed as superintendents of women prisoners was in 1883, and only recently have women prison governors been appointed to prisons. Before that a man governor with a woman deputy was the rule. The first woman governor was Miss Selena Fox, appointed lady superintendent of all sections of Aylesbury prison in 1914 and governor in 1916.

Today there are 450 women prison officers in England and Wales in a total mixed force of 15,000 – but at the end of 1971 there were only 952 women prisoners, including 282 in Borstal, as against 37,835 men. The women officers' uniforms were not given serious consideration until after World War Two and women prison governors have never worn uniforms. Their influence on the morale of woman prisoners is believed to be strengthened by the wearing of ordinary civilian clothes. But all other grades of prison officers are now in uniform.

In 1947 a tailored suit was introduced, on the lines of women's service uniforms in the recent war. It had military-style pockets, gilt rank bands on the cuffs, brass buttons and a belt, and was worn with a white shirt, stiff collar and tie and a peaked cap, later replaced by a tricorne hat, worn until 1973. Black stockings, stout laced shoes and a whistle on a visible chain completed the early outfit. By the mid-'sixties a less military suit was introduced, with a beltless, waisted jacket. A softer V-necked shirt came in and so did nylons, lighter shoes and a shoulder bag. In 1973 a new suit, on fashion lines, was introduced, with a boxy jacket with concealed fly-front fastening, slit pockets and flared skirt. An open neck shirt, a small pill-box hat, a fashionable bag and court shoes completed the outfit.

Part of the bleaker side of uniforms is their long association with prisoners, but in fact women prisoners in Britain have not worn uniform for a decade. Until the early 'sixties they did, and pictures of suffragettes, including Mrs Pankhurst and her daughter, in hideous uniforms, complete with prison arrows, are familiar. The arrows remained until the 1930s and reform did not start seriously until after World War Two. About 1947 cotton dresses in a choice of colour and in current fashion styles were introduced as uniform. About 1952 there was a further breakaway into printed dresses, and in the 1960s Viyella dresses, in many colours, were worn in winter. For outdoor exercise capes in navy wool were worn.

In 1963 the Prison Commission issued a detailed circular of instruction on the uniforms of women prisoners, announcing changes in the styles and prints of dresses and the introduction of blouses and skirts for winter. There were three designs for dresses, all made from Simplicity patterns in five sizes. The materials included floral and spotted ones.

141 The mid-'sixties uniform on smarter lines

142 Mrs Pankhurst and her daughter, Christabel, in the prison uniform of 1908

Winter blouses were in the same prints and the grey skirts could be plain or pleated. Cardigans were issued. Only the badges denoted the prisoner. How fashion was being considered is shown by the note: 'Governors are requested to report on the 1st of September, 1963, whether they consider that there has been any fundamental change in fashion to merit new patterns of dresses. If so, full particulars, including commercial (i.e. dressmaking), patterns should be submitted for consideration.'

Since 1968, however, all uniforms for women prisoners have disappeared as part of a new policy. Psychiatric care has been shown to be particularly effective for women prisoners, more than 50 per cent of whom today receive such treatment. The wearing of civilian clothing strengthens the remedial effect of this, so all women wear either their own clothing, civilian clothing chosen and bought by them in ordinary shops with Home Office funds, or, in the case of short-term prisoners, clothing supplied by the WRVS. The change is said to have greatly improved morale and in addition prison officers, now considerably involved in psychiatric care, find that the women's choice of clothes gives clues to character. The responsibilities of the prison medical service include advising on clothing. This move out of uniform for women is possible only because women prisoners, as records show, do not try to escape. Men and boys do, so that identifiable clothing is necessary.

What is generally regarded as the most glamorous of all uniformed jobs for women is that of air stewardess, or air hostess. Some of the glamour has rubbed off with the development of large-scale commercial flying, but though manifold chores may have been heaped upon her, she remains to many the golden girl of the career world of uniforms – the prettiest, the most chic, the most elegantly uniformed, the most beautifully mannered of all, impeccable in a world of falling standards of service.

Her beginnings were, however, very down to earth in character if not in the literal sense. The originator of the air stewardess was a Miss Church, a young nurse in San Francisco, who in 1930 started one of the most elegant and best known groups of women in uniform when she had the idea that airlines should 'have competent women aboard to feed aspirins to the queasy customers'. She recruited seven other nurses and they were all taken on by Boeing-United, thereby launching a new career for young women. They were known as 'the Sky Girls', and the idea spread to other American lines, TWA took on its first 23 hostesses in 1935 for the old DC-2s, all of them registered nurses aged between 21 and 26.

America had glamour-girl air hostesses before World War Two, but in Britain women first became members of plane crews in order to release men for service in the RAF or elsewhere in the armed forces. The first British girl to get her air stewardess's wings was Rosamond Gilmour, of Glasgow, who made her first flight in an Albatross aircraft flying from Whitchurch, Hampshire, to Shannon on 10 May 1943. This was a shuttle service operated by British Overseas Airways and connecting with flying boat operations.

143   The wartime air hostess's uniform

Before the end of the summer five girls were operating on the line going to Lisbon. Advertisements appeared for 30 air stewardesses. Hundreds applied, but only seven were chosen at this stage. Requirements were exacting. 'The best type for the job', said an airline official at the time, 'is the girl with the qualifications and training of an RAF nursing sister.' Discipline was strict and security was clamped down heavily on departures and routes. Food rationing made catering difficult and equipment and cabin facilities were limited throughout British Overseas Airways.

The uniform, provided by this airline, as has always been the rule, was masculine and severe, consisting of a navy blue serge suit with pleated skirt and double breasted jacket with brass buttons and a service-style shako cap. With it went a white shirt and black tie, and for serving food there was a mess jacket, also brass-buttoned. Shoes were stout black brogues and stockings gun-metal, opaque in the fashion of the time, but both were soon modified. 'Restrained make-up' and no nail varnish were specified.

The transformation of the air hostess took some considerable time and post-war uniforms remained severe and military-looking. BOAC bought surplus WRNS uniforms for their girls and service tricorne hats were worn for some time in this and other lines. But when glamour came in it knew no bounds. Girls of the French Concorde wear uniforms designed by Marc Bohan of Dior, thereby giving a boost to French couture. When British Caledonian Airways was formed in 1961 it put its girls into tartan suits, fashionable in cut, in a choice of eight authentic tartans. In 1974 long tartan skirts were introduced for wear when serving cocktails etc. National dress, like that of India and Japan, has been adopted as another means of enhancing still further the air girl's contribution to flying.

144 (*left*) Air girls follow fashion: 1947, 1954, 1960 and 1967

145 (*right*) Stepping up fashion, 1974, for all climates

146 Tartan suits on fashion lines, with matching berets

Cap designed
by Aage Thaarup

Lichen green poplin
shirt and collar,
bottle green woven tie

Skirt and jacket of
bottle green serge
designed by Norman Hartnell

Bottle green knitted
gloves with satchel
in leather to match

Nylon stockings in
" Silhouette" shade

Black leather
shoes

NUMBER ONE DRESS

147 The WRAC No. 1 dress,
introduced in 1965, designed by
Norman Hartnell: detailed
sketch

148 Mess dress for the
woman officer is high fashion.
Designer's sketch

The fact was that the publicity value of smart and fashionable uniforms had been realised. It spread to ground staff at airports. It wasn't all done in kindness. It extended to travel agents, who found that uniforms for their couriers and other members of staff who came into contact with the public served the dual purpose of ease of recognition at airports, on board ship and elsewhere, and of ensuring publicity for the company concerned. But fashion was kept in mind; Thomson Holidays in 1973 introduced a mix-and-match 'separates' wardrobe, of skirts, trousers, jackets, dresses and sweaters, in which their representatives could be suitably clad for all occasions and climates and easily recognised. Holiday camps have for years had uniformed staff; Butlins red coats are famous everywhere.

Recognition of the part women had played in the services during the war came officially in 1946, when plans were announced in Parliament to retain them in the armed forces on a permanent basis. It took three years for this to be implemented. The Women's Royal Army Corps was formed in February 1949. 'The very existence of the WRAC is a tribute to the courage and determination of women who were of assistance in times of crisis long before the Army realised their full potential', says an official publication. The motto of the WRAC is *Suaviter in modo, Fortiter in re*, 'gentle in manner, resolute in deed', and it marks a significant adjustment of attitudes between army men and women.

This was perhaps reflected when in 1963 the WRAC went out of the khaki which it had worn ever since the WAAC was formed in 1917, which it had wished on the WAAF for a time and which had been worn by many other groups of women in uniform in service contexts. The new uniform was in Lovat green, and, updated in accordance with fashion, it is the uniform which the WRAC still wears on almost all occasions. The classic suit has a single-breasted jacket with cut-away fronts, neat epaulettes and flat, slip hip pockets. The buttons carry the monogram of the late Princess Royal. The skirt is slim and a white shirt and collar and tie complete the outfit. For warm weather there is a short-sleeved casual shirt. The cap is becomingly high-crowned, with a patent leather peak. This is still known as No. 2 uniform, because a dark green formal uniform, introduced in 1965, still exists. Designed by Norman Hartnell, it is worn by high-ranking officers for ceremonial events, by the corps' bands and by its provosts, the military police section. Drivers and a few technical members continue to wear khaki as working dress.

Apart from these basics, the WRAC uniform of today is very comprehensive, amounting to more than 80 items, including a green Melton greatcoat, black gloves, a dark green shoulder bag and nylons. Black court shoes are worn. For tropical wear light weight beige linen dresses, shirt-waister style, are cool and smart.

For officers, the suit is similar but individually tailored, with ranks shown on the epaulettes and with the corps badge, a lioness surrounded by a laurel wreath, on the jacket lapels. Mess dress is the ultimate in the apotheosis of uniform into contemporary fashion, a bold step forward in a trend which has been growing steadily throughout women's uniforms. Designed by Owen Hyde-Clark, formerly of Worth, it is a slim cream and gold lamé Empire gown, with small sleeves, square neck, a fish-tail pleat at the floor-length hem and a long green silk sash fastened to the shoulder by a single rank-marked epaulette, then falling to the ground and ending in gold fringe. It is also that most rare and enviable of feminine fashions – a couture creation at less than half couture prices, made by Hilliers Couture. The WRAC stress that all their uniform is planned to be 'fashionable, smartly cut yet efficient and military in style', but the mess dress, if it is that, means a new chapter in militarism.

The strength of today's WRAC is 4,200, and it is a fully integrated part of the Army, with the same standing as any other corps. In the specialist army of our time the girls and women slot in quite naturally with specific, clearly defined functions, mainly in communications, administration and transport. There is full scope for promotion and the cadet goes to the WRAC Training College at Camberley, to emerge after eight months in her bespoke officer's uniform, which is 'kept constantly under review and changes are frequently made to keep it up-to-date and fashionable'. In many officer posts, especially administrative ones in London, uniform is, however, worn only on ceremonial occasions.

Ranks today are the same for women as men, and further training takes place at the Staff College, along with men officers. A woman can rise to be a colonel or a brigadier and director of the whole WRAC. 'There are few more satisfying and exciting careers for any girl than to be an officer in this proud and intensely feminine force', says the WRAC. 'Feminine' is startling – but significant. Today's servicewomen is not a substitute man; she has her own place alongside him.

The WRNS was also revived on 1 February 1949 as part of the peacetime structure of the Royal Navy in every respect except that its members are still not subject to the Naval Discipline Act. Uniforms have remained basically the same as during the war, but the suits of ratings are of lighter and better material. The white topped sailor hats are now worn all the year round and not only in summer, because since 1961 they have had wipe-clean plastic crowns. They are also lighter and more firmly shaped. The collar-and-tie shirt is still worn in winter, but for summer there is a short-sleeved informal shirt, white with navy piping at cuffs and collar and worn fastened at the neck with a jacket, open without. Court shoes have virtually superseded laced ones, stockings are nylons and the shoulder bag is smart. Hair has to clear the collar, make-up to be discreet. Officers' uniforms too have changed little, except in improved quality. Mess dress was introduced for them in 1951, in the form of a black ottoman rayon skirt and bolero, and a mancella blouse with gilt buttons, designed by Victor Stiebel. In 1964 today's midnight blue sleeveless dress and bolero in heavy ottoman was designed by top dress designer Jean Allen.

Today's establishment is 3,000 ratings and 250 officers. They cannot

149 Today's WRNS rating and petty officer

150   Impeccably tailored look for the WRNS officer

complain, like the sailors in the song, that they joined the Navy to see the world and all they saw was the sea, because in fact they do not go to sea at all but do go to a great many parts of the world, from Holland to Hong Kong, Malta to Mauritius, Oslo to Ottawa. They serve in 22 categories, most of them similar to those of the WRAC, but also as aircraft mechanics, meterological observers and weapon analysts. Officer cadets go to the famous Royal Naval College at Greenwich, along with naval men, but have their own courses. Royal recognition of the Service was reinforced by the appointment of Princess Anne as Chief Commandant in July 1974, with her uniform carrying one broad and one narrow pale blue ring on the sleeve, the latter marking her superiority to Commandant Mary Talbot.

The WAAF was also re-formed on 1st February 1949, as the Women's Royal Air Force, whose members were all enlisted or commissioned in the RAF with the sole restriction – a large one – that they should not undertake combatant duties. This meant that they could not fly any planes, because every flying man is regarded as a combatant, but they could be stewardesses in peacetime. In 1959, however, they were admitted to the trade of air quartermaster, which in 1962 was given air crew status. Ten airwomen were members of the first course to qualify in this way for the flying brevet on their uniforms. In 1970 the category was re-named loadmasters, as a more accurate way of describing their duties. The woman loadmaster can thus be the only woman in the crew of an RAF plane, usually in practice transport-type. From the early 1960s women have been air traffic controllers. In 1968 rank titles of women officers were brought into line with those of men in the RAF and in 1970, with the introduction of the graduate entry scheme, the first women were accepted as students at the RAF College, Cranwell. Today's WRAF women share their training and promotion with men and are promoted in competition with men.

This works in practice. There have been three women Air Commodores at once. An RAF station has been commanded by a woman. A woman engineer can be in command of a big engineering service centre. A woman aircraft controller is often in charge of a shift on a busy airfield and girl mechanics and fitters work alongside and sometimes in charge of crews responsible for the turn-round of aircraft at home and abroad.

The uniforms of WRAF women have recently been updated and, with their strong degree of equality with the RAF men, there has, paradoxically, come less emphasis on similarity between men's and women's uniforms. The same thing has happened with other women's uniforms today. Men and women are complementary in the occupations they share, so a clearer alignment with fashion and a more feminine look have come in.

The military-style jacket of the No. 1 formal WRAF uniform was done away in the 1950s, when couturier Victor Stiebel designed a flattering and smart suit which has been worn, with minor fashion changes, since then. It is neat, waisted and belted, with flat, low pockets. Officers and airwomen wear similar styles, but the officers' uniforms are individually tailored. Thereby hangs a tale. There used to be a bevy of tailors eager to make the bespoke suits, but such suits, once the pride of every well-dressed woman, are now as dead as the dodo in civilian life. The tailors have disappeared one by one and now only one main firm, Moss Bros, remains to dress the WRAF officer, who has to place her order months in advance of need and take her place in the queue. The uniform, updated as it is, is thus conforming to the time-honoured characteristic of being frozen fashion, a perpetuation of a mode discarded by the world in general. The woman officer's cap is softer than the man's, and the airwoman's wartime beret has been replaced by a becoming version of the pill-box hat, also worn by officers on informal occasions.

Where do these service uniforms come from? Until about three years ago each section of the RAF and the WRAF dealt with its own needs. This fell down as mounting costs and the rise of mass production made small orders difficult to obtain. An Assistant Directorate, Clothing Requirements and Policy, RAF, was set up under an experienced officer to look after all clothing and to co-ordinate everything from designs and contracts to production and delivery – and to ensure that colours and styles are, in fact, uniform.

One of its first big jobs was to overhaul the WRAF No. 2 working uniform. This was still the rough serge battledress top with skirt or trousers which had changed very little since 1938 and was not at all to the taste of the 1970 girl. It has now been replaced by a smart, zip-fastened boxy jacket and skirt in smooth wool and polyester, with matching trousers supplied to all. The RAF has a similar uniform. Shirts are similar for men and women, but women have an additional soft, short-sleeved summer shirt.

The biggest breakaway from traditional airwomen's, and indeed, all servicewomen's dress has been that of the loadmasters. These 50 women, plus a considerable number of ground stewardesses, wear a slim-fitting, slightly flared bright blue Crimplene dress based on a style worn by Pakistani airline hostesses. With it go matching slacks, for rough work and cold weather.

Changes of climate affect the WRAF more than other servicewomen, and a lesson from fashion has been learned in that 'layering' is adopted instead of a complete change of garments. The traveller sets off with blouse, jumper, jacket, raincoat, liner, to be removed or added one by one. A new hazard for WRAF uniform designers has been created by man-made fibres. Static electricity is a danger to those working on electric equipment; fire hazards have to be considered. Buttons can be a menace if they get into machinery and a special adhesive Velcro fastening has found unexpected usefulness in the WRAF.

Uniforms used to be thought of as worn for show, to be seen on parade, but those of the RAF and WRAF, more than most, are rarely seen. There are rows of functional garments in the wardrobes of the Clothing Directorate's 'showroom' in Holborn which are never seen away from the airfield or RAF station. But there is also the WRAF officer's elegant mess, or evening dress, Princess-style and quite a showpiece in deep blue silk and

151 WRAF officer, 1974, in bespoke tailored suit

152   A breakaway from service traditions in uniforms: the WRAF loadmaster of today

wool, with three-quarter sleeves, the badge in miniature worn as a brooch and with black or gold shoes and bag to complete the ensemble.

It could be assumed that after 40 years the FANY would not drop out of the post-war picture of women in uniform. 'The First World War brought the FANY's sphere of activity into transport and in the Second World War their most vital work was in communications', says Mrs Sheila Parkinson, head of the corps. 'Through work with the SOE, the underground, they became expert in radio-telephone and wireless telegraphy work and this dictated their post-war programme.'

One of their first moves was, however, to preserve their uniforms, by asking everyone who retired or resigned to present her uniform to them. As a result the familiar khaki military-style tunic and skirt still appear on formal occasions, such as reunions, mess nights and church parades. The supply of wartime uniforms remains adequate for all needs. For camp khaki battle dress tops and skirts are worn. The FANY blue and red colours are worn on lapels and badges, introduced in the present style in 1964.

In 1947 training in communications began, courses being started in wireless telegraphy and radio telephone work, with supplementary training in first aid (given by the RAMC), car maintenance, map reading and navigation. FANY members also learn rifle shooting and unarmed combat, both assisted by the fact that headquarters are now at the Duke of York's barracks, in Chelsea, along with various Territorial units whose co-operation is invaluable.

The spearhead of today's activities is the radio-equipped minibus acquired in 1968 by means of a fund-raising drive, to give a practical outlet for activities. A communications team helps the Metropolitan and City Police at disasters such as plane or rail crashes and fires. Some 60 members can be called on for this work by means of a round-the-clock call service.

For this work an entirely new uniform has been provided, consisting of olive green slacks of waterproof Helanca, with a matching pullover in ribbed oiled wool with the FANY shoulder flashes. A khaki FANY cap and a khaki shirt complete the outfit. For further protection there is a green anorak, hooded and wool-lined and also carrying FANY flashes.

For practical experience the minivan teams attend British Horse Show events, providing communications in cross-country events and thus harking back in a new way to their origins as women on horseback. Another new development is a service of linguists to help at non-commercial events, such as international conferences, and at hospitals. They can offer fluent speakers in ten languages. Today's members come from a wide cross-section of ordinary women. There are some 750 FANY's scattered all over the world and linked by a bi-annual news Gazette. FANY still maintains a very real corporate spirit.

When, in 1949, the Queen Alexandra nurses were given the name they now hold, Queen Alexandra's Royal Army Nursing Corps, a smart grey barathea suit was designed by Norman Hartnell as the No. 1 or 'walking out' uniform, but, as in the case of the WRAC, it is today worn only on ceremonial occasions. The ordinary outdoor uniform is a simpler grey flannel suit, similar to the normal WRAC one, with scarlet piping and epaulettes. Officers' suits are similar but individually tailored. The white poplin shirt is worn with a grey tie; the cap is grey, with a black patent leather peak; court shoes, handbag and gloves are all black.

The uniform for nursing duties is a silver-grey button-through long-sleeved dress, belted and with a soft shirt collar, with the woven QA badge on the breast pocket. For summer it is short-sleeved. For the tropics there is a white drill ward dress and a beige outdoor one, with a beige beret. Sisters and ranks above them are similarly clad, but in the wards Sisters wear the red cape, with badges of rank and white veils instead of the cap worn by nurses. The QA say of the uniform that 'the general impression is of smartness combined with femininity'. The strength of the QA's is 594 regular officers and 1,611 servicewomen (that is, not fully trained), a total of 2,215. The Territorial Army Volunteer Reserve, linked with them, consists of 288 officers and 309 servicewomen. These wear similar uniforms, but sisters do not have the red capes.

So far as the officers are concerned the QA's elegance is in the hands of people whose business it is to produce that enviable quality. Hilliers

153 (*left*) Traditional and up-to-date styles co-exist in the FANY

154 (*right*) Today's Queen Alexandra nurses' uniforms

Left: Smart grey walking out suit with scarlet-edged epaulettes worn with matching felt hat with black patent leather peak, black court shoes, gloves and handbag

Centre: For out-door duty wear in the tropics the cool beige linen dress with grey beret

Right: The nurses' ward uniform – a silver-grey button-through dress with scarlet badge on pocket, small white cap and black shoes

Couture, already mentioned, have something of a corner in dressing the top ladies in uniform and at their premises in Cork Street they employ many ex-Worth staff in their workrooms. Their managing director, Mr V. C. Petts, trained with leading couturiers Creed and Busvine and the original QA contract dates from 1940, when Hilliers began making the outdoor uniforms of the officers. After the war they added the grey ward dresses and scarlet capes. One of their staff has made 3,000 capes in the course of her career, all in superfine face cloth, sleek as a billiard table top.

A big moment in the story of nurses' uniforms, up to then in essence functional, came in 1954, when peacetime mess dress for QA officers was introduced and entrusted to Hilliers to make from a design submitted by the corps. It consisted of a long black skirt, white pin-tucked voile blouse and red satin monkey jacket. For the next ten years it was limited to officers above the rank of major. It was succeeded by a grey mess dress and then by the present style, also made up by Mr Petts from an idea suggested by the corps. It is of silver grey silk and wool, with long pure silk chiffon sleeves and a scarlet halter neckline with gold badges of rank attached to the collar. The embroidered badges have to be made in India, so fine is the workmanship required. All officers wear the mess dress on formal evening occasions. Uniform is fashion in this instance.

The other service nurses are similarly organised and uniformed, though with a much closer approximation of outdoor uniforms to those of the WRNS, and WRAF, respectively, except that members of Princess Mary's RAF Nursing Service have four-cornered hats. Naval nurses continue to wear blue cotton dresses and aprons. Sisters are in navy cotton, with aprons and navy mini-capes, piped in scarlet, and on the head the square of cotton, folded so as to form a high chignon. There are today 200 fully trained naval nursing officers and 460 in training. For RAF nurses shirt-waister dresses in white polyester strike a modern note, adopted from what was originally a tropical uniform.

It was inevitable that with the introduction of the National Health Service in 1948 the idea of a standardised uniform for hospital nurses should arise with renewed force. Nothing positive happened for some years, but in 1955 a letter to *The Times* pointed out that the abolition of nurses' caps would save the NHS £650,000 a year. This produced a prompt protest from Miss Evelyn Pearce: 'A nurse's cap is more than a sign of her office, it indicates her vocation. . . . For a very sick patient who could not possibly see a monogram on a pocket or a flash on a sleeve realises that she who comes to his bedside wearing a cap is a nurse.' A sub-committee of the Nursing Advisory Committee of the Ministry of Health, set up in 1955 to study nurses' uniforms, found stern resistance to standardisation and a fiercely protective loyalty not only to uniforms but even to the uniforms of individual hospitals. The report, published in 1959, stressed that uniforms must be smart and well-cut. 'Only the best and smartest of modern designs will do for the twentieth century professional nurse in this country', but while economy in wear, fitness of purpose, easy laundering

155   Sister and nurse of the RAF nursing service

and attractiveness must be taken into account, standardisation should not be sought nor traditions broken, because they were 'prized by the wearers, accepted and admired by the general public'. The cap was a 'badge of office' for nurses, as opposed to other hospital staff, and it should remain. New man-made materials were encouraged, but there was criticism of the 'drip-dry-droop' of the American nylon overall style of nurses' dress.

In 1966 the Ministry of Health held a uniform design competition for college of art students. A brief laid down by a working party of nurses and based on the views of 7,000 nurses and other hospital personnel specified that fine Terylene/cotton should be the material and that the dress should have front fastening, adaptable neckline, short sleeves and just cover the knees. The judges were fashion editor Ernestine Carter, designers Mary Quant and Roger Nelson and Lord Teignmouth from Hardy Amies. Winning designs were chosen, but standardised dress is as far from approval as ever. The suggestion that the seven items involved in a nurse's traditional uniform could easily be reduced to one overall has been met with a sharp riposte that this would merely resemble a cleaner's overall. One go-ahead journalist, Jean Rook, in 1966, put forward a design for a neat trouser suit as nurses' uniform, but, though echoed several times, this has got no further.

The abolition of uniforms for nurses has also been discussed, the main arguments being that the nurse would thereby gain stature as an individual and that this would not only improve relations with the patient but also help her own morale. It is a complete contradiction of the whole principle that uniforms unite and exalt the wearers, but it has been supported by some strong evidence in the area of psychiatric nursing. A

156 (*left*) New-type uniform for nurses, introduced in Vale of Leven Hospital, Scotland, in 1956. Seen here with traditional styles at a 1956 nursing exhibition

157 (*right*) Sister and nurses, St Thomas's Hospital, 1974

158   Debra Sellars, a Nightingale pupil nurse of 1974 in the modern version of the uniform

detailed survey carried out at the Royal Edinburgh Hospital showed that psychiatric patients' attitudes to their nurses improved with the abolition of uniforms, and that among the nurses concerned 'the discrepancy between ideal ratings and self ratings decreased', with benefit to morale. In general, however, the uniform has a beneficial effect both in hospitals, though not always in the increasing number of other areas of community health in which nurses are involved today.

The concept of uniform, says the London Hospital, has changed in recent years. The apron is, for instance, worn only by the bedside, and is meant for the protection of the patient, not the nurse. Outdoor uniform has almost disappeared, except for formal occasions. The traditional navy, red-lined cape is used mainly for movement from one building to another within the hospital precincts. Black stockings disappeared about 1948. Skirts got shorter, and now keep in line with fashion, though not with fashion's extremes. The biggest change in nursing and one with widespread effects not only on attitudes to it but even on its uniforms is the changing of the names of nursing staff under the Salmon Report of the mid-1960s which have taken some time to be implemented in daily practice. After centuries of religious connotation ward sisters became charge nurses; above them were nursing officers, a new grade; then assistant matrons became senior nursing officers. The matron became a principal nursing officer and above her there was for each group of hospitals a chief nursing officer. The various grades became known by numbers, charge nurses being No. 6 and the others rising one by one to PO 10. It had the advantage of integrating the ranks of male and female nurses at a time when men were increasing in numbers, but the old names linger on. It also brought in a tendency for higher grades to go out of uniform except inside hospital wards. A plain tailored suit with blouse or jersey has become the usual everyday wear for teaching and administrative staff, with a zipped white dress for visits to the wards.

In recent years the Red Cross, like other bodies concerned initially with nursing, has widened its scope to embrace welfare activities on a larger scale. The first step to this end was taken when, after the war, full membership was given not only to the trained and uniformed but also to untrained and non-uniformed helpers, previously known as associate members. In spite of this there was for a time a certain lapse from the wartime level of activity. 'To some extent,' they admit, 'the relative failure of the change to achieve the results hoped for might have been due to its being linked with a change in the Society's uniform and in uniform regulations.'

Since 1960 however, the Red Cross has been widening its scope. One official described its activities cryptically but effectively by saying: 'It plugs holes.' Wherever there were gaps in community welfare services the Red Cross would step in to fill them up. That is what it does today. The Red Cross nurse is still its best known symbol, still providing much-needed ancillary services in hospitals. She wears a short-sleeved tailored shirt-dress, knee-length, with a crisp cap perched on her modern hair style instead of the cover-up square, but she is still a very human symbol of help and assurance. On a wider scale, wars, civil disturbances, natural disasters all bring the Red Cross to the rescue, in all kinds of attire from flying kit to tropical or below-zero outfits, but always bearing that proud badge, the Red Cross emblem.

12 | Out of uniform

So far the main thread of continuity weaving its way through the story of women's uniforms has been that, except for those of servants and charity girls, all of them have in some way been indicative of a new and wider participation of women in the community, usually openly but occasionally, as in the case of the early women soldiers and sailors, disguised as men. Today, with equality of opportunity accepted at least in theory and anti-discrimination campaigns pressing it forward into actuality, women no longer need to be uniformed aggressively in order to proclaim their presence or uniformed like men to demonstrate that they have a place in a man's world. The new social picture of shared responsibilities is, however, not yet quite clearly defined; it is a multi-layered affair and this pattern is reflected in the various new trends in women's uniforms.

In general, uniforms are still worn and added to where they signify authority – in the police, the law, the armed forces and other activities where the wearer's function must be explicitly shown in the interests of public order or the general social structure and where they are acceptable because they honour the wearer. Thus, where there is a close identity of function between men and women in a particular area of activity, uniforms still tend to be generally similar, as in the police and fire services. Likewise in the services of the Crown where, though in peacetime there is considerable difference in duties, these are complementary and women have equivalent ranks and duties. Fashion has been allowed more place in this group of women's uniforms, but there is an all-over masculine influence. Tailored suits prevail and are illustrating the old thesis that uniform is frozen fashion, because they have all but vanished from today's feminine fashion. Hats and gloves remain part of formal uniform wear, though they are generally discarded by other women. But no women's service aims at copying the traditional Guards' uniforms. The Queen's single annual appearance in uniform – a feminine version of that worn by her Guards – is purely a part of the traditional ceremony of Trooping the Colour on the Sovereign's official birthday, and is out of current context, though it may be prized as an echo of the Victorian Royal ladies' emancipation into the more splendid of male uniforms for the first time in history.

Although today's Royal ladies are honorary colonels of numerous regiments and are the titular heads of many other uniformed organisations, they wear only a very few of the uniforms concerned. Princess Margaret, Countess of Snowdon, wears only two uniforms – as President of the Girl Guides and as Grand President of the St John Ambulance Association and Brigade. She wears the former when attending such things as the Annual General Meeting and visiting Girl Guide camps throughout the country; and the St John uniform is worn at the Presidents' Conference and some other events. The Duchess of Kent, as Controller Commandant of the WRAC, wears No. 2 dress in England and tropical dress when appropriate. Princess Alexandra wears only the Red Cross uniform as Vice President of the British Red Cross Society and Patron of the Junior Red Cross, but only at certain events, as frequently she has other engagements on the same day for which the uniform would not be appropriate. Princess Alice, Duchess of Gloucester, as Commandant of the WRAF, wears the uniform of Air Marshal in that force when she visits RAF stations to see members of the WRAF. She also wears the St John's uniform if she is inspecting or visiting St John's Ambulance Nursing Division. Princess Anne, as Commander in Chief of St John Ambulance Brigade Cadets, also wears that uniform when appropriate.

On the other hand, when Lance Corporal Jackie Smith of the WRAC joined the Parachute Regiment and, after two years and 471 jumps, became the first woman paratrooper, she was presented by her male colleagues among the 'Red Devils' with the red beret of the regiment and she wore the working uniform of battledress top and trousers, like a man, because she was in a man's world. Likewise, when other women have in recent times made their way into this world, working alongside men, the established similarity of uniforms has been maintained. This happened with traffic wardens, among the best-known women in uniform today and so familiar that it is difficult to realise how recent they are. The creation of a force of auxiliaries to help the police in traffic control started in 1960 with the experimental recruitment of 39 men in the Westminster area. The scheme proved effective, grew and women were recruited for the first time at Croydon in 1964. The uniform for both men and women is similar, navy with yellow hat bands, epaulettes and flashes. The women's basic outfit is a plain barathea jacket and skirt, with peaked cap, similar to the men's except for the skirt. Women have a shoe allowance to enable them to follow their own choice. Like the men, they wear shirts, with collars and ties. Four shirts and twelve collars are supplied. Six pairs of nylons are a feminine 'perk'. Of more than 30 items provided to meet all contingencies most are common to men and women. Duties are shared and include operating as traffic controllers at big public events. Today there are more than 2,000 wardens in London and, men and women alike, wardens now operate in most big cities and towns, similarly uniformed and doing similar work.

The newest of uniformed youth organisations in Britain is the Girls' Brigade, founded in 1965 but an amalgamation of three similar existing

159 HM Queen Elizabeth II: her only appearance in uniform at the annual Trooping the Colour ceremony

160 Lance Corporal Jackie Smith

161   Woman traffic warden

162   Members of today's Girls'
Brigade. Back (*left to right*)
Warrant Officer, 16 plus;
Officer, 18 plus; Brigader,
14 plus; Front: Junior, 8–10;
Explorer, 5–7

bodies, the Girls' Brigade (Ireland), dating from 1893; Scotland's Girls' Guildry, established in 1900, and the English Girls' Life Brigade, formed in 1902.

The Girls' Brigade, like all these, is a church-based organisation. It is interdenominational and international, and in Britain consists of nearly 2,500 companies, regionally organised as well as linked to headquarters, and totalling over 91,000 members. World-wide, it has nearly 174,000 members in 48 countries.

There are four categories of members, grouped according to age, and adult officers appointed by the church concerned, but trained by the Brigade. Everyone wears a navy and white uniform and the Brigade considers that its uniform 'encourages a sense of belonging and responsibility, and helps to create and maintain discipline and self-respect. It prevents barriers which can arise because of varying economic and social backgrounds.'

Pinafore dresses with jerseys and berets are the uniform of the 5 to 8 year-olds, called Explorers. For juniors, seniors, brigadiers and warrant officers, that is, girls from 8 to 18, there are navy blazers, with badges and piped with varying colours according to the group. They are worn with navy skirts, white shirts and ties and smart forage-style caps, also with the badge. Officers wear service-style tailored suits, with badges, arm-flashes, and lanyards coloured according to rank, white shirts, ties and neat felt Homburg hats, also with the badge. Overseas there are variations of the blue and white uniform to suit different climates and conditions.

Activities are aimed at encouraging mental, physical and spiritual growth and extend to games, athletics, camps, nursing, child care and community service. Members compete for Duke of Edinburgh and other awards, holds rallies, organise drama, sports and other competitions.

Other inroads by women into uniformed activities and careers previously confined to men continue to be made. The Merchant Navy has had women stewardesses for many years, wearing the uniforms of the lines concerned and today numbering over 200, but considerable progress is also being made by women into other areas of Merchant Navy work where they wear uniforms closely resembling those of the WRNS and go to sea on the same terms as their men colleagues, unlike the servicewomen of the WRNS.

These pioneer Merchant Navy women entered the service some years ago, the first company to accept a girl cadet being Denholm Ship Management of Glasgow, with which Miss Sheila Edmundson, now serving as second officer on *Benreoch*, served her apprenticeship and took her second mate's ticket. There are today about 2 or 3 Merchant Navy women officers and some 20 cadets, ten of whom took their certificates of competency in 1974, thereby becoming entitled to sail as 3rd officers with the shipping lines they trained with. Such girl cadets, selected by the British Shipping Federation and then employed directly by a shipping line, are trained exactly as boys are, doing the same work on board ship, sitting the same exams and, like the boys, receiving training and living expenses, plus a general allowance during training.

In May 1974 the first two girl cadets entered BP's new training scheme for obtaining the Second Mate's Certificate and thereby launched out into a career aboard tankers, working alongside boy cadets, sharing all duties, however rough, and wearing on formal occasions a uniform closely resembling that of the WRNS. More often they wore working clothes similar to those of their male colleagues – paint-stained blue denim dungarees, with work boots and gloves, the uniform needed for deck work and general maintenance of the ship. The course, a sandwich one including study at a marine college or school of navigation, takes two and a half years and can be combined with study for the ordinary National Certificate or Diploma in nautical science. After that girls can proceed with further studies leading ultimately to the Master's Certificate. Captain Stuart LeFevre, BP's manager responsible for cadets and their training, approves the policy. 'We consider', he says, 'that girls can perform the duties of a deck officer as well as a man. Of course, our tanker crews are used to ladies on board since all our officers can take their wives with them. We do find their presence helps to smarten a ship up as well as keeping the air less blue.' The girls fit in well with off-duty pursuits on a 'tour' of duty that averages four-and-a-half months, sometimes with a month between ports of call, and today's new seafaring girls present no problems.

Girl radio officers are also increasing in the Merchant Navy, where there are now about 20 of them, wearing similar uniforms to the others in the service. They train, however, at a Radio College, at their own expense or with the aid of local grants, then apply to a shipping company or a marine wireless company for a job. Girls have proved extremely efficient and successful in this new area of work, and shipping companies are increasing their quota of girls. Girls could also be engineer officers, there are none at present, though one did so in World War Two and became a chief engineer officer.

Girl jockeys in 1972 became eligible to race under Jockey Club rules, and therefore began to appear on race-courses wearing uniforms in the colours of the owner, as men do. In 1974 they were admitted to compete with men in races.

Lady Llewellyn-Davies became captain of HM Bodyguard of the Honorary Corps of Gentlemen-at-Arms, an office which became hers in 1974 as the Labour Government Chief Whip in the House of Lords, but it was decided by the Queen that she should wear only a badge of office and not a uniform.

Amy Johnson pioneered commercial and therefore uniformed flying for women when, in 1933, she flew de Havilland Dragons on the Paris run of a service sponsored by Edward Hillman. She was flying on the Solent Air Ferry in 1939, when the war disrupted it, and she was at first reluctant to join the ATA, saying: 'I'd much rather work in a proper commercial

163   The first two girls to work for the Second Mate's Certificate on BP tankers, in formal uniform

164   Girl jockey Meriel Tufnell after a win at Kempton Park in 1972

165   First Officer Elizabeth Overbury

aviation company with men pilots.' Even she could not achieve that and she joined the ATA, losing her life in its service. The ambition she had sought has proved elusive and the progress of women in the newest of careers has proved slow and limited. ATA pilot 'Jackie' Moggridge, determined to remain in aviation after the war, succeeded in receiving acceptance for the RAF Volunteer Reserve and in being trained as a service pilot, the only woman to do so. For the two weeks' annual camp uniform was worn and for her life in this man's world meant a masculine number and 'my uniform – slacks and battle dress – was also of masculine gender. With buttons in the wrong place.' She qualified for preliminary wings in her first year, then was promoted Pilot Officer: 'Once again I collected a uniform from Moss Bros. A sleek elegant affair of worsted and patch pockets; a pleasant change after the itchy flannel of Pilot Class IV. The thin pale-blue stripe on my sleeves was almost infinitesimal but now *I* would be addressed as Ma'am.' It led to further pioneer work as a ferry pilot, flying across the world to deliver Vampires and Spitfires to Burma, wearing RAFVR uniform. Today only a small number of women fly for commercial airlines and the national ones still remain masculine preserves. The group of women pilots is, however, distinguished and highly qualified.

Elizabeth Overbury rose to be a senior first officer with Court Line, wearing the Company's grey uniform of jacket and straight skirt, light blue shirt with epaulettes, dark blue tie, flat cap, grey raincoat, black shoes. She started flying in 1952 and, flying the de Havilland Ambassador and the Hawker Siddeley 748, was the first woman with a British airline to fly a prop-jet on scheduled services. In 1967 she achieved the most outstanding of her series of 'firsts' by becoming the first woman in the western world to fly jet passenger services.

Of three women flying for Dan Air outstanding is Yvonne Sintes, who became a captain with that line in 1972 but started her career as a BOAC air stewardess. She became the first woman air traffic controller to be employed by the Ministry of Aviation, but her ambition was to fly for an airline and in 1964 she joined Morton Air Services at Gatwick, the first British woman to be a first officer on an airline operating out of a major international airport. Joining Dan Air, she helped to inaugurate the HS 748 service. She flies as captain on 748s and has also flown as first officer on the Comet IV, for which she holds command qualifications. Her uniform, and that of her women colleagues, is based on that of the WRAF officer's jacket, worn with trousers and a WRAF officer's cap, all in Dan Air's black or midnight blue, with the company's 'wings', cap badge and appropriate rank insignia, two or four gold bands on the sleeves and epaulettes – two for first officers, four for a captain. White shirt blouses are worn, with short or long sleeves, with epaulette straps and black ties. A military style mackintosh completes the uniform.

Also with Dan Air is Delphine Gray-Fisk, currently flying as a First Officer on Comets, and Marilyn Booth, the first woman to be trained by a

166   Capt Yvonne Sintes of Dan Air

British airline. She is now flying as a first officer on the HS 748. British Air Ferries have three women on their flying staff and Britain has one woman commercial helicopter pilot, Gay Abraham. Ten women became chief stewardesses in 1974. The British Women Pilots' Association, with about 250 members, works actively to promote women's careers in aviation and the Girls' Venture Corps has air wing units, wearing an RAF blue uniform. But women still play a small part in commercial airlines – the *Flight Directory of British Aviation* contains only a handful of women's names, as against hundreds of men.

While uniforms persist where identification is necessary, there is a growing relaxation in their wear and they tend to be limited to occasions when the actual need is present. Thus the nurse's outdoor uniform is practically extinct; there is no reason for her to wear it as her uniform is purely occupational. Service men and women go out of uniform not only when off duty but also in many administrative jobs in London and elsewhere away from camps. So do men and women police and fire officers. Where there is no built-in reason for formality or for approximation to men colleagues, female uniforms are also less strict and less rigid, starting with school ones. Wartime restrictions put a brake on them until the 1950s, but from then on there were many developments, all in the direction of relaxation, and all greatly affected by the youth revolution in fashion in the 1960s. 'Domestically the fifties and sixties saw a decline of prefects and sixth form uniform, a tendency to replace prize givings by "open days", and a rising emphasis on "direct action" (task force and the like) to promote the social concerns which have always played an important part in the schools', says one report. Sixth forms went out of uniform and 'changing fashions have seen mini-skirts, maxi-coats and trouser suits. Hats have largely been abandoned, though there has been a certain revival of the "boater", regarded as rather fashionable. Black stockings, abandoned in the 1930s as terribly old-hat, have become trendy and very much "with it".'

At Christ's Hospital, under today's young headmistress, Miss E. A. Tucker, a Newnham graduate, girls go out of uniform on Saturdays, when jeans are a favourite choice. Sandals in summer, tights for the older girls, ankle and three-quarter socks for the juniors, and, for indoor games, one-piece jump suits in navy Terylene towelling, are other innovations at the oldest girls' school. For tennis there is a white jump-suit, with a white skirt over it for away games, and for outdoor games in general an A-line navy pinafore-style tunic and Aertex shirt in light blue. High on the walls of the dining room hangs a portrait of Susannah Holmes, a pupil of 1826–32, wearing the original uniform. What changes she has looked down upon since then!

The North London Collegiate School has also moved with the times, with mini-skirts and pullovers, boots and a sixth form which wears no uniform at all except on formal occasions, and is allowed complete freedom of choice, which means a strong preference for jeans and trousers of every

167 Pinafore dresses and plaid blouses become uniform for the annual parade of Christ's Hospital girls to the Mansion House to meet the Lord Mayor

kind. The effect on morale is described by the staff as wholly good: young girls like uniform and the solidarity and confidence it gives them but older ones chafe at it and it inhibits them.

But in general school uniforms remain in wide acceptance, 'retained as an important means of obliterating economic differences'. But today's educationalists see no reason why they should not follow contemporary fashion, Anoraks, slacks, sweaters have all been blessed by the GLC experts. A recent ILEA committee advised school heads to look to such items and liberate uniforms. The dividing line between uniforms and other fashions has become narrow to a degree inconceivable in the light of the history of men's uniforms.

In an egalitarian society where social distinctions have little, if any, built-in prestige, the uniforms of service have largely disappeared, starting with those of domestic servants and proceeding with the increasing laxity of uniforms worn by railway and most other transport workers, except for airlines, which still retain a certain prestigious quality reflected in elegant uniforms. Postmen and postwomen have uniforms, but in practice they show very substantial variations on the theme.

More and more women's uniformed groups are showing signs of giving up uniforms. Even among nurses this is being mooted, though feelings run high on the part of those who treasure their uniforms as a symbol of a uniquely dedicated profession. But the uniform and even the cap were challenged by Prof Jean McFarlane, appointed to the newly established Chair of Nursing at Manchester University in 1974, when a degree in nursing was introduced into Britain, following the lead previously given by the USA towards the creation of specialist, scientifically-trained nurses. In an interview which appeared in the *Daily Telegraph* Dr McFarlane declared that she thought the whole question of uniforms must be considered: 'They are an inheritance from our Army and religious background and while in some branches of nursing protective clothing is required, in others uniform is not necessary.

'I eventually see nurses going to work in their ordinary clothing so long as it is washable and the question of cross-infection is considered. A uniform can de-personalise the nurse.

'What practical use is there in the cap now worn on top of the head? It is not functional. It no longer keeps the hair in place as caps were originally intended to do. It is all part of the way we regard the nurse as a glamorous young person, an angel of mercy, and this is delaying our emergence and acceptance as highly-trained people in a science-based profession.'

In other branches of nursing and associated work uniforms are steadily disappearing, notably among Health Visitors, who today have for the most part given up the wearing of uniform, again because it tends to create barriers between them and those among whom they work.

In the religious world Quaker women began to discard uniform about the middle of last century. Formal guidance on plainness of dress was discontinued about 1860 and the distinctive garb disappeared gradually

from then, until by about 1890 it was practically never worn. 'There was a time when the Society was self-consciously following an asceticism that produced an unfortunate dowdiness, especially in the way in which women dressed', says George H. Gorman in *Introducing Quakers*. 'This has now largely passed, and while not slavishly dragooned by every whim of fashion, on the whole women Friends use make-up and dress in normal modern clothes.'

The fact that women's modern clothes were progressively becoming simpler and even more uniform-like probably contributed to a considerable degree to their adoption by previously uniformed groups. There could be little distinction between uniform and ordinary dress, as for instance in the neat grey skirts and striped blouses worn as a uniform by the girls and women of the John Lewis Partnership stores for many years and in the smart overalls worn by NAAFI girls and many shop assistants and factory workers. Sociologically too class distinctions, expressed in dress, were disappearing and regimentation of certain kinds was increasing in the community. As uniforms went out uniformity was, paradoxically, coming in – as it had done for men a long time previously in their more organised lives. It is a teasing subject for speculation on what the future will bring.

But for the purpose of this survey, the subject ends today where it began centuries ago. The women of religious orders, the first to go into uniform, were the only groups to retain that uniform without regard to fashion, and to do so for centuries, until as recently as the mid-1960s. The uniform, however, largely disappeared in Britain for some of these

168 (*left*) Woman railway porter's uniform of 1954

169 (*centre*) The postwoman's navy uniform was in 1974 replaced by a new-style grey jacket with skirt or slacks

170 (*right*) London Transport's 1974 uniform for on the buses

centuries, because at the Reformation such religious orders were broken up and either disappeared or else fled to the Continent, where one group, founded in the Low Countries at this time, moved around so fast and so much that they became known as 'the galloping gurls'.

The revival and modern growth of female religious orders began after the French Revolution and most of those in existence today were formed between 1800 and 1870. Sisters of Charity, founded about 1650 by St Vincent de Paul, were an exception; they were not enclosed and were not nuns to their generation because 'the streets were their cloister', so that they could not make the vows of religion but made vows which were renewable yearly. As recently as 1949 Princess Andrew of Greece, mother of Prince Philip, founded a Christian Sisterhood of Martha & Mary, with grey monastic full-flowing robe and coif, which she invariably wore.

All groups on their foundation were united in looking backwards in time for their distinctive habits or uniforms, which were either medieval or else based on traditional peasant dress. Typical is the Society of the Sacred Heart of Jesus, a 7,000-strong, nearly world-wide group, whose dress on its foundation in 1800 in France was based on that of a Burgundian widow. The long loose robe, cloak and bonnet with a goffered frill and a long veil were in a style that dated back at least 300 years. The Order spread to America in 1818 and to Britain in 1842. A notable American, Cornelia Connelly, who spent some time with the Sacred Heart Sisters, founded the Society of the Holy Child Jesus in the USA in 1850.

The first move to change the all-embracing adherence to the past was made in 1961, when the Vatican Council met for the first time since 1870, when its deliberations had been cut short by the Franco-Prussian War, with the result that the only decisions reached related to the position of the Pope. When Pope John called the Council in 1961, among the subjects discussed in a crowded conclave at St Peters was the religious life and whether it was appropriate to modern life that any section of it should live in the style of 300 years ago, as nuns still did. The orders were advised to review their life-style in relation to the charisma of their founders and to modify, change or abolish what was out-of-date or unnecessary in the light of today's apostolate. The result was a revolution in the dress and way of life of nuns. It was urged that on grounds of health, hygiene and practicability the old attire, with its cumbersome, engulfing garments, should no longer be enforced, though it was agreed that those who wished to retain it could do so. The younger nuns spearheaded the move towards lighter clothing, easy-care materials and to the decisions, made by many Orders, acting autonomously, that lay dress, in contemporary fashion, could be worn. So could modern uniforms, if preferred, the style being sometimes dictated by the major superior and her court, in others by the Sisters themselves, who were left free to choose what to wear. Some orders went completely out of uniform, while others wore an agreed modern design, usually a dress and jacket or skirt and jacket, worn with a beret or plain hat. For formal occasions a short veil was worn. One group, the Sisters of

Charles de Foucauld, elected to wear a long blue denim dress with leather belt and sandals, thus achieving a close resemblance to the current 'hippy' dress!

Today only a few older nuns cling to the traditional habit. The others go about their work among the people dressed like the people. They are usually called Sister, but sometimes use the description 'Miss'. They keep their own names. There are practical as well as sociological reasons for modern dress, because nuns drive cars, go to universities, train teachers and therefore are Government employees who have to go out and about on official duties. In more detail, the old headdress interfered with glasses; close caps were bad for the hair; goffering them took an hour and a half apiece.

Sister Honor Basset, a retired teacher and an Oxford graduate in history, has been a nun since 1927 and wore the old-style habit for nearly 40 years. Now she wears modern lay dress and feels that it is beneficial to do so. Like Sir Mortimer Wheeler, she believes that uniforms and regimentation can lower the individual's standards by making the observance of rules the only criteria of conduct and personal integrity. 'Uniforms have some advantages,' she admits, 'but in this present world it is better not to wear them.' They can create barriers in the work of service in the community, they can inhibit communications and sometimes frighten children.

Women's uniforms started as a means of distinguishing particular groups dedicated to service. In a society like that of today, based on a belief in universal human rights and therefore on acceptance of universally shared responsibilities, the question of uniforms assumes a new dimension. Today's nuns move among the people without distinction or barrier. They can go to restaurants, go home for holidays, pay visits to friends, fitting their religious duties into the life-pattern they plan as individuals in the community. It is the end of the basic need for uniforms, perhaps the exit line of the whole subject, or at any rate in that area of it concerned with the fabric of everyday life. The uniforms of pomp and circumstance, pride and glory, ceremonial and display, are another matter, part of a tradition to which women have not made any independent contribution. Up to the present they have either stood apart or else followed or adapted those of men when admitted to the ceremonies, honours or vocations concerned. Whether they will continue to accept this masculine lead is a question it would be rash to attempt to answer.

Bibliography

Abel-Smith, Brian, *A History of the Nursing Profession*, Heinemann, 1960
  The Hospitals, 1800–1848, Heinemann, 1964
Adams, Samuel and Sarah, *The Complete Servant*, Knight & Lacey, 1825
Adburgham, Alison, *A Punch History of Manners and Modes 1841–1940*, Hutchinson, 1961
Austin, Anne L., *History of Nursing Source Book*, Portman, New York, 1957
Balfour, Lady Frances, *Elsie Inglis*, Hodder & Stoughton, 1918
Barnes, Major R. M., *A History of the Regiments and Uniforms of the British Army*, Seeley Service, 1950
Bayne-Powell, Rosamond, *The English Child in the Eighteenth Century*, Murray, 1939
Beale, Dorothea, *History of Cheltenham College, 1853–1904*, Cheltenham, 1904
Beauman, Katharine Bentley, *Partners in Blue*, Hutchinson, 1971
Beeton, Isabella, *Mrs. Beeton's Book of Household Management*, Ward Lock, 1861; New Edition, 1888
Berckman, Evelyn, *The Hidden Navy*, Hamish Hamilton, 1973
Bigland, Eileen, *Britain's Other Army: The Story of the A.T.S.*, Nicholson and Watson, 1946
  The Story of the W.R.N.S., Nicholson and Watson, 1946
Blackstone, G. V., *A History of the British Fire Service*, Routledge & Kegan Paul, 1957
Bott, Alan and Clephane, Irene, *Our Mothers*, Gollancz, 1932
Bradbrook, Muriel C., *That Infidel Place: A short history of Girton College 1869–1969*, Chatto & Windus, 1969
Braddon, Russell, *Nancy Wake*, Cassell, 1956
Brett, W. I.., *A Short History of Nursing*, Faber, 1960
Brittain, Vera, *Testament of Youth*, Gollancz, 1933
  Lady into Woman, Dakers, 1953
Burstall, Sara, *English High Schools for Girls*, Longmans, 1907
  The Story of the Manchester High School for Girls, Manchester UP, 1911
  Retrospect and Prospect: Sixty Years of Women's Education, Longmans Green, 1933
Calder, Jean McKinley, *The Story of Nursing*, Methuen, 1954
Cito-Malard, Suzanne, *Religious Orders*, Trs G. Robinson, Burns & Oates, 1964
Clark-Kennedy, A. E., *Edith Cavell*, Faber, 1965
Collett-Wadge, D., *Women in Uniform*, Sampson Low, 1947
Cook, Sir Edward, *Life of Florence Nightingale*, Macmillan, 1913
Cox, Mary, *British Women at War*, Murray & Pilot Press, 1941
Cunnington, C. Willett, *Women*, Burke, 1950
Cunnington, C. Willett and Phillis, *Handbook of English Mediaeval Costume*, Faber, 1952
  Handbook of English Costume, Black, 1960
Cunnington, Phillis and Lucas, Catherine, *Occupational Costume in England, from the 11th Century to 1914*, Black, 1967
Curtis, Lettice, *The Forgotten Pilots*, Foulis, 1971
Cuthbert, B. W., *The History of the Women's Branch of the Fire Service 1938–1944*, Home Office, 1947, Privately printed
Dalgardo, Alan, *As they saw Her: Florence Nightingale*, Harrap, 1970
Defoe, Daniel, *The Life and Adventures of Mrs. Christian Davies, commonly called Mother Ross*, Peter Davies, 1928

Drummond, John D., *Blue for a Girl: The Story of the W.R.N.S.*, W. H. Allen, 1960

Gardiner, Dorothy, *English Girlhood at School*, OUP, 1929

Gathorne-Hardy, Jonathan, *The Rise and Fall of the British Nanny*, Hodder and Stoughton, 1972

Gibbs-Smith, Charles H., *Aviation*, HMSO, 1970

Girls' Public Day School Trust, *A Centenary Review*, GPDST, 1972

Goldsmith, Margaret, *Women at War*, Lindsay Drummond, 1943

Gorman, George H., *Introducing Quakers*, Friends Home Service Committee, 1974 (revised reprint)

Gosden, P. H. J. H., *How they were Taught*, Blackwell, 1969

Gribble, Francis, *Women in War*, Sampson Low, 1916

Grierson, Janet, *Isobel Gilmore*, SPCK, 1962

Gwynne-Vaughan, Dame Helen, *Service with the Army*, Hutchinson, 1942

Haldane, Elizabeth, C. H., *LlD: The British Nurse in Peace and War*, Murray, 1923

Hargreaves, R., *Women-at-Arms*, Hutchinson, 1930

Harrison, Ada (Editor), *Grey and Scarlet*, Hodder & Stoughton, 1944

Heath, Sophie May (Lady) and Wolfe-Murray, Stella, *Women and Flying*, J. Long, 1929

Hecht, J. Jean, *The Domestic Servant Class in Eighteenth Century England*, Routledge & Kegan Paul, 1956

Hobman, D. L., *Go Spin, you Jade!*, Watts, 1967

Hole, Christina, *English Home Life*, Batsford, 1947

Jaeger, Muriel, *Before Victoria*, Chatto & Windus, 1956, Penguin Books, 1967

Kamm, Josephine, *How Different from Us*, Bodley Head, 1958
  Hope Deferred: Girls' Education in English history, Methuen, 1965
  Rapiers and Battleaxes, Allen & Unwin, 1966
  Indicative Past, Allen & Unwin, 1971

Kemp, Peter, *The British Sailor*, Dent, 1970

Kent, John, *Elizabeth Fry*, Batsford, 1962

Laffin, John, *Women in Battle*, Abelard-Schuman, 1967

Lamb, Felicia and Pickthorn, Helen, *Locked-up Daughters*, Hodder and Stoughton, 1968

Laughton Mathews, Vera, DBE *Blue Tapestry*, Hollis & Carter, 1948

Laver, James, *British Military Uniforms*, Penguin Books, 1948
  A Concise History of English Costume, Thames and Hudson, 1969

Lawrence, Margot, *Shadow of Swords*, Michael Joseph, 1972

Lemprière, W., *A History of the Girls' School of Christ's Hospital*, Cambridge UP, 1924

Leslie, Anita, *Jennie*, Hutchinson, 1969

Liddell, Alex, *The Girl Guides, 1910–1970*, Muller, 1970

Lister, Margot, *Costumes of Everyday Life; a History of Working Clothes from 900–1900*, Barrie & Jenkins, 1972

Lumsden, Louisa Innes, *Yellow Leaves*, Blackwood, 1932

MacBride, Vonla, *Never at Sea, Life in the W.R.N.S.*, Educational Explorers, 1966

McLaren, Barbara, *Women of the War*, Hodder & Stoughton, 1917

Manton, Jo, *Elizabeth Garrett Anderson*, A. & C. Black, 1956
  Sister Dora: The Life of Dorothy Pattison, Methuen, 1971

Marshall, Dorothy, *The English Domestic Servant in History*, G. Philips for the Historical Association, 1949

Miller, Harry, *Service for the Services: The Story of N.A.A.F.I.*, Newman Neame, 1971

Mitchell, David, *Women on the Warpath*, Cape, 1966

Moore, Doris Langley, *The Child in Fashion*, Batsford, 1953

Morgan, M. C., *Cheltenham College: The First Hundred Years*, R. Sadler, 1968

Mosley, Sir Oswald, *My Life*, Nelson, 1968

Nightingale, Florence, *Notes on Nursing*, Harrison, 1860

North London Collegiate School 1850–1950, OUP, 1950

O'Malley, Ida, *Florence Nightingale, 1820–1856*, Thornton Butterworth, 1931

Page, Frances Mary, *Christ's Hospital*, G. Bell, 1953

Peck, Winifred, *A Little Learning*, Faber, 1952

Percival, Alicia C., *The English Miss Today and Yesterday*, Harrap, 1939

Pike, E. Royston, *Human Documents of the Age of the Forsytes*, Allen & Unwin, 1969

Pinchbeck, Joy and Hewitt, Margaret, *Children in English Society: Tudor Times to the Eighteenth Century*, Routledge & Kegan Paul, 1969

Power, Eileen, *Medieval English Nunneries*, CUP, 1922

Powell, Margaret, *Below Stairs*, Peter Davies, 1968

    The Treasure Upstairs, Peter Davies, 1970

Quennell, Peter, *Samuel Johnson, his Friends and Enemies*, Weidenfeld & Nicolson, 1973

Racster, Olga and Grove, Jessica, *Dr. James Barry: Her Secret Story*, Gerald Howe, 1932

Rae, Isobel, *The Strange Story of Dr. James Barry*, Longmans Green, 1958

Raikes, Elizabeth, *Dorothea Beale of Cheltenham*, Constable, 1908

Red Cross, *The Proudest Badge*, British Red Cross Society, 1972. (6th Edition)

Richardson, Samuel, *Pamela*, J. Weeks, Halifax 1814. (pub. 1741)

Ridley, Annie E., *Frances Mary Buss*, Longmans Green, 1895

Rudofsky, Bernard, *The Unfashionable Human Body*, Hart-Davis, 1972

Robinson, Victor, *White Caps*, Lippincott, 1946

Sackville-West, V., *The W.L.A.*, Michael Joseph, 1944

St. Leonards School 1877–1927, OUP, 1927

Scott, Peggy, *British Women in War*, Hutchinson, 1940

Scott-Thomson, Gladys, *The Russells of Bloomsbury, 1669–1771*, Cape, 1940

Seymer, Lucy Ridgely, *Florence Nightingale*, Faber, 1950

    A General History of Nursing, Faber 1949 (3rd Edition) 1954

Stack, Prunella, *Life is Movement*, Collins, 1973

Steadman, Florence Cicely, *In the Days of Miss Beale*, E. J. Burrow, 1931

Strachey, Ray, *The Cause*, G. Bell, 1928

Stuart, Dorothy Margaret, *The Girl Through the Ages*, Harrap, 1933

    The English Abigail, Macmillan, 1946

Sykes, Christopher, *Nancy*, Collins, 1972

Trimmer, Mrs S., *The Oeconomy of Charity*, Vol. 2, J. Johnson & F. & C. Rivington, 1802

The W.A.A.F. in Action, A. & C. Black, 1944

Ward, Baroness, *F.A.N.Y. Invicta*, Hutchinson, 1955

Wilkins, Frances, *Six Great Nurses*, H. Hamilton, 1962

Wilkinson, Frederick, *Battle Dress*, Guiness Signatures, 1970

Wise, Terence, *A Guide to Military Museums*, Model & Allied Publications, 1971

Woodham-Smith, Cecil, *Florence Nightingale*, Collins, 1951

Woods, Reginald (Editor), *Harvest of the Years*, Salvationist Publishing & Supplies, 1960

Woolley, Hannah, *The Complete Serving Maid*, Passinger, 1677

Zouche, Dorothy E. de, *Roedean School, 1885–1955*, Private, 1955

Periodicals

Girl of the Period Miscellany, 1869, 342, Strand

Illustrated London News, July–December 1854

The Girls' Realm, Vol. 8, May 1906, S. H. Bousfield

The Times History of the War, Vol. IV, The Times, 1915

The Nursing Mirror

The Nursing Times

Index